how2become

GCSE English is Easy: Shakespeare – Romeo & Juliet

Discussion, analysis and comprehensive practice questions to aid your GCSE. Achieve 100%

www.How2Become.com

As part of this product you have also received FREE access to online tests that will help you to pass GCSE English assessments

To gain access, simply go to:

www.MyEducationalTests.co.uk

Get more products for passing any test at:

www.How2Become.com

Orders: Please contact How2Become Ltd, Suite 3, 40 Churchill Square Business Centre, Kings Hill, Kent ME19 4YU.

You can order through Amazon.co.uk under ISBN: **9781912370214**, via the website www.How2Become.com or through Gardners.com.

ISBN: **9781912370214**

First published in 2018 by How2Become Ltd.

Typeset by Katie Noakes for How2Become Ltd.

Disclaimer

Every effort has been made to ensure that the information contained within this guide is accurate at the time of publication. How2Become Ltd is not responsible for anyone failing any part of any selection process as a result of the information contained within this guide. How2Become Ltd and their authors cannot accept any responsibility for any errors or omissions within this guide, however caused. No responsibility for loss or damage occasioned by any person acting, or refraining from action, as a result of the material in this publication can be accepted by How2Become Ltd.

The information within this guide does not represent the views of any third party service or organisation.

CONTENTS

GCSE ENGLISH PREP

GCSE ENGLISH LITERATURE EXAM STRUCTURE

Your GCSE Literature examination is comprised of **two** sections:

Paper 1: Shakespeare and the 19th Century Novel

Marks out of 64

1 hour and 45 minutes

40% of GCSE

Paper 2: Modern Texts and Poetry

Marks out of 96

2 hours and 15 minutes

60% of GCSE

This book will focus on the Shakespeare section of Paper 1.

Assessment Objectives

AO1 = To read, understand, and respond to literary texts. Students should be able to demonstrate a critical style in their writing, and develop an informed personal response. Students are also required to use contextual references, including quotations, in order to support their interpretation.

AO2 = To analyse the language, form, and structure used by an author and analyse the meaning and context. To ensure relevant terminology is used throughout their assessment.

AO3 = To show an understanding of the relationships between texts and the contexts in which a piece of text is written.

AO4 = To use an array of vocabulary and sentence structures in order to provide clarity, purpose and effect, with accurate spelling and punctuation.

Weighting of Assessment Objectives

Below we have outlined the weighting of assessment objectives for your GCSE English Literature exam.

AOs	Paper 1 (approx)	Paper 2 (approx)	Overall weighting (approx)
AO1	15	22.5	37.5
AO2	15	27.5	42.5
AO3	7.5	7.5	15
AO4	2.5	2.5	5
Overall weighting of components	40%	60%	100%

BREAKDOWN OF ASSESSMENTS

Before you begin preparing for each section of your GCSE English Literature exam, we think it is important that you understand what to expect in terms of subject content, and how to make the most out of your revision time.

Shakespeare

During the Shakespeare section of your English Literature exam, you will be required to answer **ONE** question.

Students will study one play within the classroom, and therefore, the choice of question you should answer should be the one you have been focusing on during your English lessons.

In the exam, there will be a choice of six possible Shakespeare plays. The following texts are examples taken from the 2017 examination:

- *Macbeth;*

- *Romeo and Juliet;*

- *The Tempest;*

- *The Merchant of Venice;*

- *Much Ado About Nothing;*

- *Julius Caesar.*

PLEASE NOTE: The choice of Shakespearean texts is subject to change annually. Be sure to check with your teacher with regards to the Shakespeare text that you will be studying!

The 19th Century Novel

During the 19th Century novel section of your English Literature exam, you will be required to answer **ONE** question.

Students will study one novel within the classroom, so the choice of question you should answer should be the one you have been focusing on during your English lessons.

In the exam, there will be a choice of seven novels. The following texts are examples taken from the 2017 examination:

- *The Strange Case of Dr Jekyll and Mr Hyde;*

- *A Christmas Carol;*

- *Great Expectations;*

- *Jane Eyre;*

- *Frankenstein;*

- *Pride and Prejudice;*

- *The Sign of Four.*

PLEASE NOTE: The choice of 19th Century texts are subject to change annually. Be sure to check with your teacher with regards to the novel that you will be studying!

Modern Texts

During the modern text section of your English Literature exam, you will be required to answer **ONE** question.

Students will study one text within the classroom, so the choice of question you should answer should be the one you have been focusing on during your English lessons.

In the exam, there will be a choice of twelve texts, including post-1914 prose and drama. The following texts are examples taken from the 2017 examination:

PROSE

Author	Title
William Golding	Lord of the Flies
AQA Anthology	Telling Tales
George Orwell	Animal Farm
Kazuo Ishiguro	Never Let Me Go
Meera Syal	Anita and Me
Stephen Kelman	Pigeon English

DRAMA

Author	Title
JB Priestley	An Inspector Calls
Willy Russell	Blood Brothers
Alan Bennett	The History Boys
Dennis Kelly	DNA
Simon Stephens	The Curious Incident of the Dog in the Night-Time
Shelagh Delaney	A Taste of Honey

PLEASE NOTE: The choice of modern texts is subject to change annually. Be sure to check with your teacher with regards to the novel/ play that you will be studying!

Poetry

During the poetry section of your English Literature exam, you will be required to answer **ONE CLUSTER OF POEMS** in the exam.

The poems assessed in the exam will be taken from the AQA poetry anthology, Poems Past and Present.

In the exam, there will be a choice of two clusters, each containing 15 poems. The poems in each cluster are thematically linked.

The themes provided for the 2017 examinations were the following:

* *Love and Relationships;*

* *Power and Conflict.*

For this section of the exam, students need to study all 15 poems in their chosen cluster and be prepared to write about any of them in the exam.

PLEASE NOTE: The choice of poetry texts and themes are subject to change annually. Be sure to check with your teacher with regards to the poems/themes that you will be studying!

Unseen Poetry

The unseen poetry section of your English Literature exam is self-explanatory. This section will provide poems of which you will not have studied during your English lessons.

The best way to revise for the unseen poetry section is to experience a wide range of poetry and develop the following analytical skills:

CONTENT	THEMES
LANGUAGE	STRUCTURE

GCSE ENGLISH GRADES 9-1

As of 2017, the GCSE grading system for the English subject uses a 9-1 scoring criteria.

Based on this new scoring system, students should be aiming for a Grade 9 – the highest possible grade, currently set at a higher level than what an A* used to be.

By 2019, all GCSE subjects will use this new and improved grading system with the hope to provide more differentiation between students' scores.

Below we have provided a diagram outlining the new 9-1 grading system, just to give you some insight into how this compares to the old A*-U grading system.

Average %	85+		69-84	46-68		32-45	15-31	Under 15
New grading system	9	8	7	6	5	4	3	
Old grading system	A*		A	B		C	D	E

PLEASE NOTE: the above scoring system does not necessarily reflect the actual grading system of all exam boards and should be used as a guideline only. It is recommended to check with your exam board for their exact scoring system.

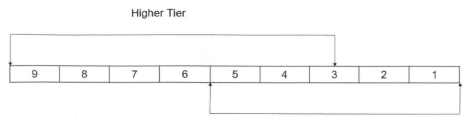

Higher Tier

| 9 | 8 | 7 | 6 | 5 | 4 | 3 | 2 | 1 |

Foundation Tier

UNDERSTANDING SHAKESPEAREAN PLAYS

THE WORKS OF SHAKESPEARE

WHO WAS WILLIAM SHAKESPEARE?

William Shakespeare was a British poet and playwright, and is still considered one of the greatest writers in literary history.

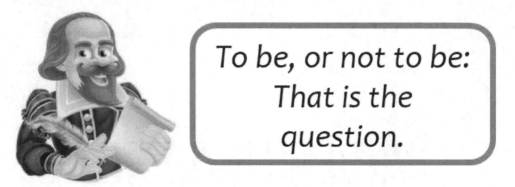

To be, or not to be:
That is the
question.

SHAKESPEARE AND HIS WORK

Shakespeare wrote around 40 plays, 154 sonnets and a whole range of other poetry about 400 years ago (1564-1616).

Some of his most well-known plays include:

ROMEO AND JULIET	MACBETH	JULIUS CAESAR
A MIDSUMMER NIGHT'S DREAM	OTHELLO	THE TAMING OF THE SHREW
MUCH ADO ABOUT NOTHING	KING LEAR	HAMLET

The works of Shakespeare are taught in schools as a way of recognising writing that is in an old-fashioned style.

Due to the time in which Shakespeare was writing (over 400 years ago), his writing style was very different to how we read and write today.

Shakespeare's works were able to capture the interest of his audience using conflict and emotion.

LIVING IN SHAKESPEAREAN TIMES

Obviously, there are many differences between the era in which Shakespeare was writing, and now.

Shakespeare's writing was heavily influenced by what life was like at that time. This enabled him to appeal to his audiences, by conveying imagery and values which were recognisable.

The key areas that Shakespeare paid particular attention to when writing are listed below.

GOVERNMENT

- For the majority of his life, Shakespeare grew up writing under the reigning monarch of Queen Elizabeth I.

- King James I ruled after her.

RELIGION

- England was a Christian country.

- Almost everyone believed in God and went to church.

- Many people believed in witchcraft, magic and ghosts.

- No-one divorced in this era.

WOMEN

- Women had no rights.

- They had to obey what their father (and/or husband) told them.

- Women had no career opportunities.

- They were often forced into arranged marriages.
- Even if the woman was the eldest, the first eldest brother would inherit everything.

EDUCATION

- Boys (from the age of 4) would go to school to learn to read and write.
- They would also learn prayers, teachings of the Church, and working with numbers.
- Grammar schools would focus on Latin, translations and writing.
- Girls would stay at home and learn to be domesticated (cook, sew, music). Only a few girls would learn to read and write.

HEALTH

- Diseases were prominent around the city of London.
- The Black Death (also known as the Plague) wiped out thousands of civilians.
- Many children died from the disease, including Shakespeare's son, Hamnet.

CLASS

- At the time of writing, society was divided into different classes.
- These classes defined people's wealth and status, which ultimately formed a hierarchy which people would follow.
- The nobles (considered the very richest of people) were called 'lords' and 'ladies'. They were the ruling class, which had influence over what the monarchy did.

- Just beneath the nobles, were the gentry. These people were rich enough to survive off their own wealth, but did not have titles within society.

- Shakespeare himself was raised as a middle class citizen. The middle class consisted of yeomen, merchants and craftsmen. Whilst they were not wealthy, they lived comfortably, and their children would have gone to school.

- The lower class worked for the superiors in society. The lower class had little money, but were still able to attend the theatre.

FEATURES OF SHAKESPEARE'S WORK

Shakespeare used a range of literary techniques in order to appeal to his readers/audiences.

There are three main areas that you should focus on when reading Shakespeare:

- *Language;*

- *Characters;*

- *Themes.*

LANGUAGE

Many people struggle to understand the works of Shakespeare, because his writing style and language is extremely different to ours.

The use of old-fashioned language made it difficult for readers to interpret, but these words and phrases were often worked out by understanding the rest of the script.

For example:

The below extract is the opening from Othello.

RODERIGO

Tush, never tell me! I take it much unkindly	*Don't try and make me believe that*
That though, Iago, who hast had my purse	*Have*
As if the strings were thine shouldst know of this.	*Talking about the elopement.*

Getting used to the language is difficult, but with more practice, this will become easier.

Remember, you don't have to understand every word in order to understand what is being said. Some of the words are simply missing letters, whilst others are words that you might not have heard of!

You will need to be able to translate what is being said, in order to analyse what is being said.

<u>Some things to look out for:</u>

Words that you may not recognise or used in a different context to how it would be used today.

Thy	→	Your	Art	→	Are or skill
Hath	→	Has	Hence	→	Away

The language used was often quite 'wordy'. Words and phrases were often swapped around which makes it tricky to work out what is actually being said.

When you read Shakespeare's plays, it is important to read straight into the next line (unless there is a full stop or other punctuation mark).

In a lot of Shakespeare's works, he used poetic devices in his dialogue. Poetry was often spoken by the characters who were wealthy, whereas slang and normal language were spoken by the commoners.

Shakespeare used language to emphasise religious, biblical, medical, legal and sexual references.

> Full fathom five thy father lies;
> Of is bones are coral made;
> Those are pearls that were his eyes:
> Nothing of him that doth fade
>
> *The Tempest*

CHARACTERS

Characters play a crucial role in the works of Shakespeare. They are often conveyed to the audience in a particular way, in order to create different emotions and ideas about each character.

When you read about characters, you need to consider the following:

- *How do they act?*
- *What is their role in the narrative?*
- *What do they get up to?*
- *How do they speak?*
- *What are their relationships like with other characters?*
- *How does Shakespeare want you to feel about that character?*

Take a look at the representation of a few characters from *Romeo and Juliet*:

CHARACTER	REPRESENTATION
Romeo	• Impulsive, immature, devoted, passionate
	• His dialogue towards Juliet is very poetic, deep and meaningful

Juliet	• Naive, innocent, devoted
	• Lack of freedom
	• Shows courage and independence
Friar Lawrence	• Friend to both Romeo and Juliet
	• Civic-minded
	• Tries to create union between the two families
The Nurse	• Sentimental character
	• Confidant to Juliet
	• A comical character

THEMES

What is the play about? What is the overall theme of the play?

Shakespeare wrote loads of plays, each of which focussed on different key themes. These themes were all considered relevant to the time in which Shakespeare was writing.

There are three types of Shakespearean plays:

1.   Comedies

2.   Tragedies

3.   Histories

Comedies

• This is a different type of humour than what we find funny in today's world.

• Most Shakespearean comedies offer dramatic storylines, alongside their underlying humour.

• Most comedies offer a happy ending.

Characteristics = struggle of young love, element of separation, mistaken identities, interwoven plotlines, use of puns and irony, and family conflict.

Tragedies

- Tend to be more serious, dramatic and tense.

- Usually involve death of main character/s.

Characteristics = social breakdown, isolation of main characters, ends in death, noble characters who are brought down by their flaws, and no escape from the drama.

Histories

- Focus on English monarchs including King John, Richard II, Henry VIII and loads more.

- Dangers of civil war and conflict.

- Present a particular image of monarchs, although often considered as misrepresentations and inaccurate.

Characteristics = use of English monarchs to centre the storyline, glorify ancestors, depict monarchs in a particular way, and use conflict and tragedy to dramatise the narrative.

Below we have listed some common themes that appear across the works of Shakespeare.

LOVE	FORBIDDEN LOVE	FAMILY	FRIENDSHIP
MORALS	RELIGION	RIVALRY	HONOUR
INNOCENCE	REVENGE	FATE	JUSTICE
SLAVERY	MAGIC	BETRAYAL	FORGIVENESS

Generally, plays will have more than one theme running through the narrative.

Some themes may be more obvious than others.

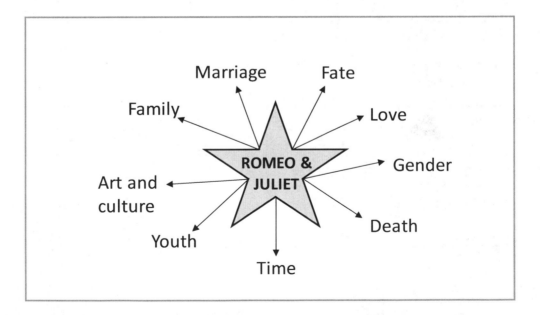

AUDIENCES

William Shakespeare's works appealed to the majority. Just like today, ticket prices were based on whereabouts you sat.

Shakespeare wanted to target a mass audience, from merchants and nobles, to poorer people.

When it comes to reading the works of Shakespeare, it is important that, as the reader, you are able to understand how Shakespeare appealed to his audience.

In his works, Shakespeare used language, imagery, themes, characters and narrative to appeal to his targeted audience. We will look at each of the aforementioned in more detail.

THEATRE PERFORMANCES

As we all know, plays are meant to be performed. So when reading Shakespeare's plays, keep in mind that they are meant to be performed on stage.

This will allow you to analyse the play in more detail, highlighting how this would have been effective for a Shakespearean audience.

The folllowing is a list of facts that you should try to remember for your GCSE exam:

INTERESTING FACTS!

- If the audience didn't like the play, they would throw apples at the actors.

- Women were not allowed to act. All female roles were played by men. This is evident in Shakespeare's comedies, as he often references this in a jokey manner.

- The costumes for the plays were often quite elobarate to highlight the fashion of that time.

- The settings of play were often kept minimalistic to ensure that they were easily adapted for each scene.

- The only person who didn't go to the theatre was Queen Elizabeth I.

- People who stood to watch the play are called 'groundlings'. In the summer, they would be referred to as 'stinkards'.

- Merchants would buy tickets to sit in the boxes next to the stage.

- Nobles would buy seats on the stage because they could be seen by everyone.

SHAKESPEAREAN LANGUAGE

Of course, we cannot provide you with all of Shakespeare's unusual Elizabethan words. However, we thought we would provide you with some of the most popular words and translations, in order to become familiar with the kind of language Shakespeare used.

We have also provided space for you to fill in words yourself to see whether or not you are able to translate old-fashioned English into modern-day English. As you read through works of Shakespeare, if there are any words you are unsure of, write them down and get a friend, parent or teacher to help you translate it.

Remember to use this glossary when revising to ensure you know what Shakespeare is talking about.

MODERN DAY	ELIZABETHAN
Afraid	Afeard
Aware	Acknown
Away	Hence
Banished	Banish'd
Before	Ere
Beg	Pray
Chase (romantically)	Woo
Come here	Come hither
Curse	Plague
Days	-morrow
Desire	Will
Does	Doth
Enemy	Foe
Escaped	'scap'd
Farewell	Adieu

Go	Hie
Go away	Avaunt
Has	Hath
Have	Hast
Here	Hither
Indeed	Marry
Inferiors	Sirrah
I think	Methinks
It is	'tis
Ignore	Shun
Kill	Dispatch
Listen	Hark
Misery	Woe
Never	Ne'r
No	Nay
Nothing	Nought
Often	Oft
Order	Charge
Pay attention	Mark
Quickly	Apace
Remember	Bethink
Sad	Heavy
Soon	Anon
There	Thither
To which	Whereto
Were	Wast
Why	Wherefore
Wished	Wish'd
Yes	Aye

You	Thou; thee
You are	Thou art
You should	Thou should'st
Your	Thy

MODERN DAY	ELIZABETHAN

Now that we have provided some example of Shakespearean words and phrases, let's take a look at some key literary techniques.

When talking about the above literary techiques, consider:

- *Why the author has chosen to use the technique?*

- *What impact does this have on the reader/audience?*

- *What does this say about the character?*

- *How does this impact the narrative?*

Let's take a look at an example:

> Romeo's emotive speech towards Juliet clearly emphasises the importance of love and desire. When Romeo uses the rhetorical question of "did my heart love till now?" this shows how Shakespeare often uses poetry techniques to highlight the power of love between the protagonists.

THE IMPORTANCE OF HUMOUR

When analysing language, Shakepeare often uses humour in his works. Puns and jokes are often demonstrated in the hope to keep with the theme of the story, relieve tension and drama, and to lighten and uplift the mood of the reader/audience.

Let's explore this idea further using a couple of examples:

> In Romeo and Juliet, when Romeo asks Mercutio how badly wounded he is, he says "Tis not so deep as a well, nor so wide as a church-door, but 'tis enough, 'twill serve... Ask for me tomorrow, and you will find me a grave man." Mercutio's use of the word "grave" not only suggests how serious his wounds are, but also signifies the resting place of the dead. His jokey language about his own death demonstrates Shakespeare's humour to help lighten the mood.

SHAKESPEARE'S USE OF POETRY IN DRAMA

Another technique that Shakespeare often applies to his works is to use poetry techniques in his plays.

Things to look out for:

1. Do the character's speech change between prose and poetry?

2. Remember, if a new line starts with a capital letter it is **VERSE**, if it continues from the last line, it is **PROSE**.

When you quote verse, it is important that you show that the quote continues over a line using the slash symbol '/'.

EXERCISE

For the following headings, make notes using the text and examples to support your answer.

CHARACTERS

THEMES

CONTEXT AND SETTING

LANGUAGE

Consider the following:

- Why are they important?

- What impact do these have on an audience/reader?

INTRODUCTION TO ROMEO AND JULIET

INTRODUCING THE CHARACTERS

ROMEO MONTAGUE

JULIET CAPULET

THE MONTAGUES

THE CAPULETS

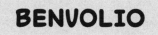

BENVOLIO

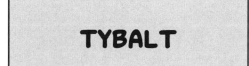

TYBALT

Here's your chance to have a go at drawing the other characters in the play based on what you THINK they would look like.

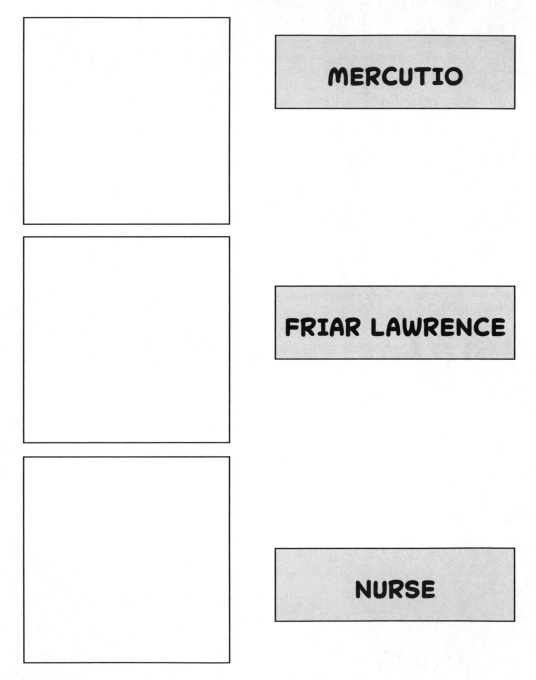

MERCUTIO

FRIAR LAWRENCE

NURSE

Here's your chance to have a go at drawing the other characters in the play based on what you THINK they would look like. Think about the characters Paris and The Prince.

OTHER CHARACTERS

PLOT SUMMARY

Romeo and Juliet is one of Shakespeare's most well-known tragic love stories. A couple that falls in love, despite their social backgrounds and family feuds, is driven to a tragic ending when their forbidden love leads to their deaths.

When analysing *Romeo and Juliet*, you need to be able to recap the main events of the play. In this section of the guide, we have broken down the play into the main events to hopefully give you a better insight into what the play is about.

ACT ONE - The Ball

- Amongst two rival families, a fight breaks out between them. The Prince demands them to stop, otherwise they'll be sentenced to death.

- Romeo is unhappy in his relationship with Rosaline. Romeo tells his friend Benvolio that their relationship is not built on love.

- Juliet's father decides to throw a fancy-dress party. Romeo gate-crashes the party with his friend, Benvolio.

- Act One sees Romeo and Juliet meet for the very first time. They fall in love at first spite, oblivious to their family rivalry.

- Towards the end of the party, Romeo finds out that Juliet is a Capulet, and Juliet finds out that Romeo is a Montague.

ACT TWO - Romeo and Juliet get married in secret!

- Romeo sneaks in to the Capulet's garden. Juliet is standing at her window talking out loud about her feelings for Romeo.

- Romeo and Juliet decide to get married.

ACT THREE AND FOUR - Two real deaths and one fake death

- Tybalt (Juliet's cousin) kills Romeo's friend, Mercutio, in a fight.

- Out of revenge, Romeo kills Tybalt.

- The Prince banishes Romeo from the city.

- Romeo and Juliet spend the night together.

- Juliet's parents tell Juliet that she is to marry Paris, despite already being married to Romeo.

- Juliet and the Friar come up with a plan to fake her own death. The plan is for Romeo to receive a letter from the Friar to rescue her after the potion wears off.

- Juliet is believed to be dead and her family bury her in the family tomb.

ACT FIVE - A tragic ending

- Unfortunately, Romeo does not receive the Friar's letter. He too believes Juliet is dead. He goes to her tomb to kill himself.

- Romeo kills Paris.

- Romeo lies next to Juliet and drinks poison.

- As Juliet wakes, she realises that Romeo is dead.

- Juliet kills herself.

- Everyone arrives at the tomb, and the Friar explains what's happened.

- The rivalry between the Montagues and the Capulets is put to rest, after realising their family feud has caused the death of their children.

AT THE TIME OF WRITING...

The time in which something is written is crucial in its story telling and ideologies.

We have briefly discussed some of the main features that were important when Shakespeare was writing. For these details, go to page 20, for an in-depth analysis of context, including:

- Government;

- Religion;

- Women;

- Education;

- Health;

- Class;

- Language.

To be watched not to be read

When we discuss the background of *Romeo and Juliet*, is is important to understand how the play was intended.

When reading *Romeo and Juliet*, you should bear in mind that it is a play. Shakespeare intended this play to be watched, rather than read. A play acts out the story that is being told, which not only makes it easier to follow, but makes analysing the written text a lot more complex.

You need to read the text with the understanding of how this would be acted out. If you try to read it like a story, you are likely to get confused. A great way to improve your understanding of the play is to watch a play. Even watching a film version of the play will help you gain clarification as to what the story is about.

The importance of theatre

During Shakespearean times, there was no TV, radio or internet. Their main form of entertainment was theatre productions. The theatre was a form of entertainment that allowed everyone from all walks of life to enjoy. From the poorest to richest and even the Queen enjoyed going to the theatre.

Bear in mind that at the time in which *Romeo and Juliet* was written, women were not allowed to act. The roles of women in plays were played by young boys or men. This clearly ties in with how men and women were represented in this era.

The Globe Theatre in London is associated with the works of Shakespeare. It was originally built in 1599 and was rebuilt in 1997.

CHARACTER ANALYSIS

CHARACTER ANALYSIS

ROMEO

Along with Juliet, Romeo is the central figure in the play. Throughout the play, the character of Romeo portrays a number of different characteristics.

Below we have highlighted major characteristics that you should learn in relation to Romeo's character. We have written the first two characteristics using explanations and evidence. Can you explain and find evidence for the others?

Characteristic	Explanation	Evidence
Romantic	Talks a lot about love	"Love is a smoke made with the fume of sighs"
Respected	He is considered to be respected by other characters	"a virtuous and well-governed youth"
Moody		
Lonely		

Characteristic	Explanation	Evidence
Funny		
Intelligent		
Dangerous		
Hot-headed		
Immature		
Honest		

EXERCISE

Can you think of any other characteristics that sum up Romeo's character?

ROMANCE   PASSION   CONFLICT   FAMILY   FATE

JULIET

Juliet is the other main protagonist of the play. Shakespeare represents her character in very particular ways using imagery, themes and context.

Below we have highlighted major characteristics that you should learn in relation to Juliet's character. We have written the first two characteristics using explanations and evidence. Can you explain and find evidence for the others?

Characteristic	Explanation	Evidence
Beautiful	Imagery of nature and light is used to represent her beauty	"the brightness of her cheek would shame those stars"
Romantic	She is also represented as being a hopeless romantic	"my love as deep: the more I give to thee / the more I have, for both are infinite"
Brave		
Independent		
Young		
Innocent		

Characteristic	Explanation	Evidence
Determined		
Foolish		
Rebellious		
Impulsive		
Passionate		

EXERCISE

Can you think of any other characteristics that sum up Juliet's character?

ROMANCE   PASSION   YOUTH   TIME   FATE   DEATH

THE MONTAGUES

The Montagues refer to Romeo's mother and father. Lady Montague and her husband are extremely contrasting characters.

Below we have highlighted major characteristics that you should learn in relation to the Monague family. We have written the first two characteristics using explanations and evidence. Can you explain and find evidence for the others?

Characteristic	Explanation	Evidence
Violent	Montague is represented as angry and violent	"Thou villain Capulet! - Hold me not, let me go"
Peaceful	Lady Montague is represented as a peaceful character	"Thou shalt not stir one foot to seek a foe"
Loyalty		
Honour		
Emotional		
Family-orientated		

THE CAPULETS

The Capulets refer to Juliet's mother and father. Lady Capulet and her husband are extremely contrasting characters.

Below we have highlighted major characteristics that you should learn in relation to the Capulet family. We have written the first two characteristics using explanations and evidence. Can you explain and find evidence for the others?

Characteristic	Explanation	Evidence
Ambitious	Lady Capulet is represented as ambitious	"share all that he doth possess"
Unforgiving	Lady Capulet is not a forgiving character	"we will have vengeance for it"
Unsympathetic		
Violent		
Unmotherly		
Controlling		

BENVOLIO

Benvolio is Romeo's cousin. He is portrayed as being a peaceful character.

Below we have highlighted major characteristics that you should learn in relation to Benvolio's character. We have written the first two characteristics using explanations and evidence. Can you explain and find evidence for the others?

Characteristic	Explanation	Evidence
Kind	Benvolio is often represented as kind	"What sadness lengthens Romeo's hours"
Peaceful	Benvolio can be considered as one of the most peaceful characters	"I do but keep the peace, put up thy sword"
Family-orientated		
Peacemaker		
Trustworthy		
Counselor		

TYBALT

Tybalt is Juliet's cousin. He is portrayed as having a strong hatred for the Montagues, and is always seen to be causing havoc.

Below we have highlighted major characteristics that you should learn in relation to Tybalt's character. We have written the first two characteristics using explanations and evidence. Can you explain and find evidence for the others?

Characteristic	Explanation	Evidence
Aggressive	Tybalt is seen to be one of the most aggressive characters in the play	"...talk of peace? I hate the word"
Troublemaker	Tybalt is a troublemaker	"[Tybalt under Romeo's arm stabs Mercutio]"
Loyal		
Honour		
Confrontational		

MERCUTIO

Mercutio is related to the Prince and is Romeo's best friend.

Below we have highlighted major characteristics that you should learn in relation to Mercurio's character. We have written the first two characteristics using explanations and evidence. Can you explain and find evidence for the others?

Characteristic	Explanation	Evidence
Mocking	Mercutio is mocking towards other characters	"rat-catcher" "King of Cats"
Talkative	Mercutio is a talkative character	"Peace, peace, Mercutio, peace. Thou talk'st of nothing"
Lively		
Honour		
Down-to-earth		
Intelligent		
Witty		

FRIAR LAWRENCE

Friar Lawrence is to that of a monk. The Friar hands out potions and plants which contain special powers.

Below we have highlighted major characteristics that you should learn in relation to the Friar's character. We have written the first two characteristics using explanations and evidence. Can you explain and find evidence for the others?

Characteristic	Explanation	Evidence
Respected	The Friar is a respected character	"O Lord, I could have stayed here all the night / To hear good counsel"
Wise	The Friar is a wise character	"Love moderately; long love doth so"
Sensible		
Confidant		
Trustworthy		
Holy man		
Father-figure		

THE NURSE

The Nurse is Juliet's nanny. She looks after Juliet.

Below we have highlighted major characteristics that you should learn in relation to the Nurse's character. We have written the first two characteristics using explanations and evidence. Can you explain and find evidence for the others?

Characteristic	Explanation	Evidence
Caring	As a nurse, she is represented as caring	"Thou wast the prettiest babe the e'er I nurs'd"
Affectionate	The Nurse has affectionate names for Juliet	"lamb" "ladybird"
Vulgar		
Opinionated		
Mother figure		
Irresponsible		
Humour		

OTHER CHARACTERS

There are lots of other characters in *Romeo and Juliet*. These characters don't appear too much, but still play a role in the play.

- PARIS

Characteristic	Explanation	Evidence
Respectful	Paris is represented as respectful towards Juliet	"The gallant, young, and noble gentleman"
Polite	His character is represented as kind and polite	"But now my lord, what say you to my suit"

- THE PRINCE

Characteristic	Explanation	Evidence
Authorative	The Prince brings authority over the rivalling families	"Throw your mistemper'd weapons to the ground"
Political power	He is a figure of political power	"And for that offence / Immediately we do exile him hence"

- THE SERVANTS (BALTHASAR AND PETER)

Characteristic	Explanation	Evidence
Loyal	The servants are loyal to the family they serve	"It doth so, holy sir; and there's my master"
Illiterate	Peter is shown to be illiterate	Peter is unable to read the names listed on the invite to the Capulet's party

SUMMARY AND ANALYSIS OF ACTS

ACT ONE

This section gives you analysis of Act I of *Romeo and Juliet*.

The Prologue

Romeo and Juliet uses a 14 line prologue to introduce the play,.

> The prologue acts as a great way to introduce the main themes of the play. During the prologue, the audience are made aware of the feud between two families — the Montagues and the Capulets.
>
> The prologue provides information as to where the play takes place, and introduces the main protagonists. The prologue suggests that the protagonists, Romeo and Juliet, are "star-cross'd lovers" which highlights that their relationship was doomed right from the offset.

The fact that the prologue is written in 14 lines suggests that Shakespeare is bringing an element of poetic devices to the play. This tehcnique is often used when writing sonnets. The use of sonnets in this play highlight the main theme of love.

The use of the prologue helps:

• Set the mood and atmosphere for the rest of the play. From the offset, we are subject to a story that is going to explore ideas of love, drama and tragedy.

• Highlight the main themes of the play – love, hate, rivalry, conflict, family, honour and death.

| LOVE | DEATH | FATE | CONFLICT | FAMILY | HONOUR |

Act I Scene I

- The first scene sees a sword fight between the two rivalry families – the Capulets and Montagues.

- The idea of conflict at the beginning of the play implies how this theme is key to *Romeo and Juliet*.

- Prince Escalus enters demanding the fight to stop. He says that the next person to cause any trouble will be executed.

- In Scene I, Romeo is portrayed as being upset because he loves a girl called Rosaline, who doesn't love him back. This suggests that Romeo is not only a romantic, but an emotional character.

> In Act I Scene I, the character of Tybalt is portrayed as a violent, active, and troublesome character. Shakespeare conveys this at the beginning of the play, so the audience take his character as someone who is going to cause conflict throughout the play.

Act I Scene II

- In Act I Scene II, Paris asks for permission to marry Juliet. The Capulets ask him to be patient because she is only thirteen.

- He is given permission to "woo" Juliet. The masked ball is the perfect opportunity to do this.

- Romeo and Benvolio decide to gate crash the Capulets party, because Romeo knows Rosaline will be there.

- The characters of Rosaline and Paris contrast with the characters of *Romeo and Juliet*. Romeo and Juliet are shown to be a lot more passionate and romantic compared to Rosaline and Paris.

In Act I Scene II, the concept of love is explored in very different ways through the use of different characters. Romeo and Juliet are both portrayed as romantics. However, Paris and Rosaline are represented in a very different light.

Juliet's relationship with Paris suggests that this type of love would be for financial gain. This is reitterated by Juliet having to "share all that he doth possess".

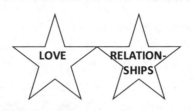

Act I Scene III

- Juliet's confidant, The Nurse, rambles on about a story about her late husband and how he use to make inappropriate sexual jokes about Juliet, despite only being thirteen.

- Lady Capulet tells Juliet about Paris' plans to marry her. Juliet is hesitant, but agrees to consider Paris at the masked ball.

- Paris is described as being beautiful. The Nurse talks of Paris as "a man of wax". Lady Capulet compares him using nature by stating "Verona's summer hath not such a flower". Both of these imply Paris to be of perfection.

LOVE   MARRIAGE   FAMILY

Act I Scene IV

- The Capulet's are throwing a masked ball, which Romeo and Benvolio are not invited to (they are Montagues). This creates suspense... something is obviously going to kick off.

- Romeo is still pining over Rosaline. Mercutio tries to distract Romeo with a story about Queen Mab, a fictitious elf who infiltrates men's dreams. This mythical imagery creates a spooky atmosphere, which compliments the theme of suspense.

- Romeo admits having a dream which has made him concerned about attending the Capulet's party.

> In Act I Scene IV, Shakespeare uses the literary technique of foreshadowing to highlight future events. Romeo's dream which has made him apprehensive to attend the ball foreshadows that something bad is going to happen. This instantly creates further tension for the audience/reader.

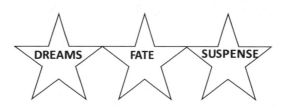

DREAMS   FATE   SUSPENSE

Act I Scene V

- This is a key scene in the play. Romeo enters the masked ball and sees Juliet for the very first time. The idea of love at first sight is explored.

- Romeo approaches Juliet and touches her hand. Oblivious to the fact that they are from rivalling families, they speak in sonnet and Romeo kisses her.

- Romeo discovers that Juliet is a Capulet, and as the party winds down, Juliet discovers that Romeo is a Montague. Juliet is heartbroken as she has fallen in love with a "loathed enemy".

- This scene ends on a great deal of suspense. The audience are left wondering how and whether or not their relationship will continue.

When Romeo and Juliet speak for the very first time, Shakespeare uses poetic techniques to explore the theme of love. Shakespeare uses a sonnet to show how Romeo and Juliet's language go hand-in-hand. Their language blends together perfectly which signify that they are a perfect match. Shakespeare also uses religious imagery such as "this holy shrine" and "holy palmer's kiss" to show how much the characters worship one another.

LOVE   CONFLICT   SUSPENSE

ACT TWO

This section gives you analysis of Act II of *Romeo and Juliet*.

The Prologue

- Act Two begins with a prologue which recaps the story so far.

- This prologue is written as a sonnet. It uses the poetic technique of rhyming couplets to emphasise the love between Romeo and Juliet.

The prologue is used to recap the main events of Act One. This allows the audience to get a break from the intense and emotional atmosphere, and focus on the key points of what has happened so far. Prologues are a fantastic way to provide context and background details in order to sum up the main themes, characters and plotlines.

Act II Scene I

- Act II Scene I is a short scene. Mercutio and Benvolio look for Romeo out on the streets. Mercutio uses lots of obscene wordplays such as "I conjure thee by Rosaline's bright eyes" and "quivering thigh".

- Mercutio and Benvolio eventually give up looking for Romeo and return home.

> Mercutio's language in this scene is used to show opposition between his character and Romeo's. Romeo's character is often described as being romantic, whereas Mercutio is represented as being slightly crude and less passionate.

FAMILY   FRIEND-SHIP

Act II Scene II

- Act II Scene II is another key scene in the play. This is commonly known as 'the balcony scene'.

- Romeo leaps over the Capulet's garden wall and hides beneath Juliet's balcony.

- Juliet's speech is a soliloquy. She talks to herself about her feelings for Romeo, but he overhears everything she says.

- Romeo interrupts her and confesses his love for her.

- Juliet suggests that they should get married, despite their family rivalries.

> Shakespeare uses a soliloquy to allow Juliet to speak opely about her feelings, allowing both the audience and Romeo to overhear her thoughts. This scene is pivotal as it demonstrates their impulsiveness and romance.

The fact that Romeo promises to get their marriage sorted to by the next day reinforces their impulsive decisions. This also allows this scene to move at a rapid pace.

LOVE   MARRIAGE   TENSION

Act II Scene III

- In this scene, we are introduced to Friar Lawrence.

- The Friar is represented as a kind and wise man.

- Romeo asks the Friar to marry him to Juliet. The Friar agrees.

- The relationship between Romeo and the Friar appears to be sincere and close. The Friar refers to Romeo as "young son" reitterating their closeness.

- Although the Friar is doubtful about the sincerity of Romeo's feelings towards Juliet, he agrees to marry them in order to order to resovle the family feuds between the Montagues and the Capulets.

- Shakespeare uses the character of Friar Lawrence to foreshadow many events to come in the story. For example, the Friar states that plants and weeds can be used to cure and to misuse as poison. This foreshadows the poison used to fake Juliet's own death and Romeo's actual death.

The Friar agrees to help Romeo secretly marry Juliet. This suggests that the Friar is using this opportunity to turn the Montagues and Capulets hatred towards one another into admiralty.

The fact that Romeo and Juliet have to marry in secret reinforces this idea of their relationship being doomed right from the offset.

FRIEND SHIP   SECRECY   LOVE

Act II Scene IV

- Tybalt sends a challenge to duel with Romeo.

- Romeo sends a message to Juliet (via the Nurse) informing her that their wedding has been arranged.

- Romeo fools around with Mercutio and Benvolio and tease the Nurse.

- Time is a clear theme in this Act. The fact that Romeo states that him and Juliet are to be married at 2pm (in less than 24 hours) illustrates the speed in which their relationship is progressing.

Act II Scene V

- Juliet waits for the Nurse to return. She is frustrated because she's been left waiting for over three hours. She accuses the Nurse of being slow.

- The return of the Nurse and Peter sees Juliet eager to find out more information. Juliet tells the Nurse to send Peter away.

- The comical language between the Nurse and Juliet show the closeness of their relationship. The Nurse states that she is aching and is very tired.

- The Nurse teases Juliet by making her wait for the news. The Nurse informs her to go and see Friar Lawrence, who will wed the two.

When the Nurse tells Juliet the news, Juliet's face turns red – "Now comes the wanton blood up in your cheeks". The redness in Juliet's face could suggest that she is thinking about her wedding night. This highlights the change in Juliet's character from being represented as young and naive, to a mature woman.

Act II Scene VI

- The final scene in Act II is very short, and is just before the wedding happens.

- The shortness of this scene suggests that Shakespeare is trying to convey to the audience how rushed the whole thing is. Romeo and Juliet's relationship has been rushed right from the beginning, and these short scenes are a great way to reitterate this idea of time, or lack of.

- The Friar is represented to be caring and friendly in this scene. He has Romeo's best interests at heart. He suggests Romeo not to be in such a rush and should shy away some of his emotions.

> When the Friar warns Romeo about his emotions being too apparent, this suggests danger. The Friar states "these violent delights have violent ends" which foreshadow the tragic ending of Romeo and Juliet's short-lasting relationship.

LOVE   TIME   FATE

ACT THREE

This section gives you analysis of Act III of *Romeo and Juliet*.

Act III Scene I

- This is another key scene for you to remember!

- Mercutio, Mercutio's servant and Benvolio are walking the streets of Verona.

- Benvolio sees the Capulets and warns Mercutio to be careful. Although Mercutio is ready for a fight.

- Tybalt wants to fight Romeo. Mercutio begins teasing him, and they both begin to fight.

- Romeo intervenes and tries to put a stop to the conflict.

- Romeo's loyalties are torn at this point. Of course he wants to protect his best friend Mercutio, but he also needs to protect Tybalt because he is Juliet's cousin.

- Tybalt kills Mercutio. This makes the scene dramatic. The audience are subject to watch a likeable, funny character come to a tragic ending.

- From this point, Romeo seeks revenge on Tybalt. Romeo fights and kills Tybalt. This is turning point in the action. Romeo is banished from the city by the Prince. This causes suspense because the audience are left wondering how his relationship with Juliet will continue.

This pivotal scene in Romeo and Juliet signifies the sheer conflict that is apparent between two rivalling families. The families will stop at nothing in order to maintain honour and gain revenge. Shakespeare's writing allows the audience to see this conflict through numerous characters, at numerous times throughout the play. This reinforces how conflict is one of the major themes surrounding the play.

CONFLICT   DEATH   HONOUR   REVENGE   LOYALTY

Act III Scene II

- After the pivotal scene, the audience are left hanging after Tybalt's death and Romeo's banishment.

- Juliet is unaware of what has happened and waits for Romeo in her room to spend their wedding night together.

- Juliet will be torn between the love of her true love, and the love and grief felt towards her cousin, Tybalt.

- The Nurse comes in and Juliet tries to find out where Romeo is.

When Juliet asks the Nurse what's wrong, she responds with "he's dead, he's dead". Juliet presumes she is talking about Romeo.

- Juliet believes that Romeo is dead. Her thoughts are suicidal at this point.

- Juliet finds out the truth about what has happened. Juliet's emotions are all over the place.

- Although she thinks Romeo is evil, she still loves him. She decides to stand by her husband.

This scene clearly emphasises how Juliet's character is torn between familial loyalty and her loyalty towards her new husband. The fact that Juliet chooses to stand by her husband shows that she has chosen Romeo over Tybalt, and more importantly, her family.

This signifies the strength of love between Romeo and Juliet, and despite the audience thinking that they might have jumped into things far too quickly, the audience can see how their love is powerful and indestructible.

FAMILY   CONFLICT   LOYALTY   LOVE

Act III Scene III

- Romeo believes that there is no place in the world for him except in Verona. He tells the Friar that his banishment from the city equates to the same outcome as death.

- In this scene, the audience see Romeo becoming suicidal.

- For the first time, the audience sees the Friar's agressive side. He tells Romeo that he's being ungrateful and that the Prince is being merciful in his decision with banishing him from the city.

- The Friar convinces Romeo not to kill himself.

- When Romeo leaves, his attitude takes a dramatic turn. He becomes ecstatic at the thought of seeing Juliet. Shakespeare clearly wants to portray Romeo as having severe mood swings.

There are a lot of ities between this Act and Act III, Scene II. In this scene, Romeo becomes suicidal by the thought of living without his beloved Juliet. The audience have already had this idea conveyed to them when Juliet was suicidal in the thought of Romeo being dead.

This ity allows the audience to see that Shakespeare has carefully thought about his imagery and how he uses this to create imagery between the main protagonists.

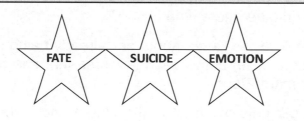

FATE   SUICIDE   EMOTION

Act III Scene IV

- Juliet's father is talking to Paris and says that Paris and Juliet are to be married on Thursday.

- Lady Capulet tells Paris that she will find out in the morning as to whether Juliet will agree to marry him. This is dramatic irony. The audience know that Juliet is already married and therefore cannot be married again.

- This is another turning point in the action. Juliet is set to be married to Paris, despite already being married to her family's rivalry.

MARRIAGE   LOVE   DUTY

Act III Scene V

- Romeo and Juliet have their wedding night.

- Early next morning, Romeo says that he "must be gone and live or stay and die". This signifies that he needs to leave for Mantua.

- After a prolonged goodbye, Romeo leaves.

- The scene changes dramatically from romantic to aggressive. Capulet is outraged when he finds out that Juliet has refused to marry Paris. Capulet thinks Juliet is illogical and stupid, and states that he will drag her there if he has to.

- Juliet confides to the Nurse about her already being married, and seeks comfort. Juliet convinces the Nurse that she has changed her mind to marry Paris.

- She no longer puts her trust in the Nurse and instead will seek advice from the Friar.

In historical context, daughters are expected to obey their fathers. The fact that Juliet is shown to be disobedient towards her father, shows how Shakespeare tries to break free from typical Elizabethan traditions.

This contrasts with the beginning of the scene where the audience see Romeo and Juliet's relationship blossoming. Their love for one another is shown through romantic imagery ("light" and "day") and rhythmic language ("grows" and "woes"). This shows how both characters understand eachother's rhythms and pace.

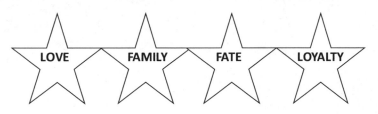

LOVE   FAMILY   FATE   LOYALTY

ACT FOUR

This section gives you analysis of Act IV of *Romeo and Juliet*.

Act IV Scene I

- The Friar and Lawrence are talking about Juliet. Juliet then enters the scene. Despite her feeling suicidal and angry, she has to be polite to Paris.

- When Paris leaves, Juliet expresses her feelings to the Friar. Friar tells Juliet to put down the knife.

- The Friar comes up with a plan to fake her own death. He hands her a potion and tells her to go home and pretend to be happy. She is then told to drink the liquid Wednesday night which will make it look like she is dead.

- When Juliet 'appears' to be dead, the Friar will send a letter to Romeo to come and take her away and live together in Mantua.

The Friar is subject to help Juliet as much as he can. He is a religious man and therefore he cannot allow her to marry for a second time – this would be sinful. The fact that the Friar is responsible for her secret marriage to Romeo, suggests that he will do everything in his power to help Juliet out of this conflicting situation.

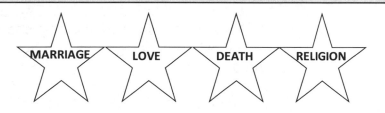

MARRIAGE   LOVE   DEATH   RELIGION

Act IV Scene II

- In this scene, the audience see Juliet playing the dutiful daugher, going along with the marriage preparations to Paris.

- Juliet's father has made a list of people to invite to the wedding. He hands this list to a servingman.

- Lord Capulet changes the marriage day from Thursday to Wednesday. This means that Juliet must drink the sleeping potion one night before she and the Friar had planned.

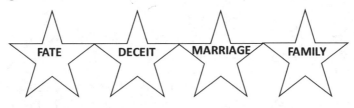

FATE   DECEIT   MARRIAGE   FAMILY

Act IV Scene III

- Juliet is in her bedroom. She prepares to take the sleeping potion that the Friar gave to her.

- Juliet contemplates whether the potion will work or not. Is the potion a way for the Friar to kill her so he doesn't get into trouble about her actual marriage to Romeo and her proposed marriage to Paris?

- Juliet's soliloquey is used to say "farewell". She speaks about the tomb in which she will lay – a "foul mouth" and "festering" place where Tybalt's body lies.

- Juliet's character deteriates at this point by thinking she sees the ghost of Tybalt. With his ghost threatening to kill Romeo, she drinks the potion. She falls onto the bed.

> Shakespeare uses this soliloquey for the audience to understand the final thoughts and feelings Juliet is suffering with. This is Juliet's last big speech in the play, and therefore is significant in addressing the change in her character, highlighting her emotional and physical decline. At this point, the audience sympathise with her character.

Act IV Scene IV

- The wedding plans are well underway, and Capulet, Lady Capulet and the Nurse are preparing the house for Juliet's wedding.

- This scene contrasts significantly to the events in the last scene. This scene appears jolly and everyone is in a good mood.

- This scene mirrors Scene V in Act I, when the Capulets were preparing for the ball. This shows how the play has progressed in a short amount of time, and how romance is leading to a tragic end.

MARRIAGE   FAMILY   FATE

Act IV Scene V

- The Nurse discovers Juliet, who appears to be sleeping. She soon realises that Juliet is dead, although the audience know that she's not.

- When the Capulets and Paris are told about Juliet's death, they all appear to be upset. This shows that they did love Juliet despite their disagreements.

- Peter tells the musicians to play something cheerful. This is somewhat bizarre given the tragic circumstances, but Shakespeare could be providing a rest period for the audience to deal with all the ups-and-downs in emotion.

FAMILY   LOVE   DEATH

ACT FIVE

This section gives you analysis of Act V of *Romeo and Juliet*.

Act V Scene I

- Meanwhile, amongst all the events taking place in Verona, Romeo is in Mantua dreaming about his love for Juliet.

- Romeo dreams that he dies and that she brings him back to life with a kiss. This foreshadows what's to come, although Juliet's kiss is unable to revive him.

- Romeo's servant tells him that Juliet is dead.

- Romeo has not received the letter that the Friar had sent, and therefore he thinks that Juliet really is dead.

- Romeo gets his hands on some poison so that he can kill himself and lie with Juliet in the tomb.

The moment when Romeo finds out that Juliet is dead (supposedly), he instantly wants to end his life. This shows that he would do anything, even death, to be by the side of the woman he loves.

Although the letter did not arrive, Romeo's impatience is another reason for his downfall. His foolishness and inability to be patient, leads him to make a hasty decision and kill himself. Had he held on a little longer, he would have realised that Juliet's death was fake, and that their fate could have been saved.

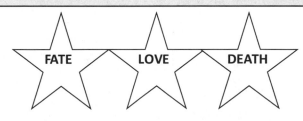

FATE   LOVE   DEATH

Act V Scene II

- A turning point in the action is seen in this scene when the audience find out that the Friar's letter was not delivered to Romeo. Therefore, Romeo is oblivious to Juliet's and the Friar's plan. This makes the Act even more tense.

- Friar Lawrence's plan has spiralled out of control. He rushes to the Juliet's tomb.

- The Friar is unaware that Romeo is also on his way to Verona to kill himself after the news of Juliet's death.

- Despite knowing how the play is going to end, the audience are hopeful that all will work out. However, we all know from the prologue that this play has a tragic ending.

FATE   LOVE   DEATH

Act V Scene III

- Scene III in Act V is probably the biggest scene so far.

- Paris and his servant go to Juliet's tomb. When Romeo arrives with his servant, Paris decides to hide.

- Romeo tells his servant to leave and take a letter to his father.

- Paris is watching Romeo. He thinks he is about to vandalise the tomb, so Paris tries to arrest him.

- Although Romeo does not want to fight, Paris doesn't cave in and they fight. Romeo kills Paris. Paris' final words were to lie next to Juliet. This implies that he did actually love Juliet.

- Romeo looks at Juliet and thinks that their fate is to be together, and the only way this can be achieved now is through death.

- Romeo drinks the poison. As he dies, he says "Here's to my love".

- Friar Lawrence enters and finds Paris and Romeo's bodies.

- Juliet wakes to discover that the Friar is standing before her. He runs away.

- Juliet sees Romeo and kisses his lips, hoping that some of the poison he drunk remains on his lips.

- Juliet finds Romeo's dagger and stabs herself.

- The townsguards, the Prince, Capulet and Lady Capulet arrive at the tomb. The Watch explain what has happened, and that Paris, Romeo and Juliet are dead.

- The majority of the characters are on stage. Everyone learns about the deaths and the prince blames the family feuds for the deaths of everyone – Romeo, Juliet, Mercutio, Tybalt and Paris.

- The Capulets and the Montagues decide to make peace and put up a stature in memory of Romeo and Juliet.

- The conflict between the families finally ends.

The tragedy finally ends with the deaths of both Romeo and Juliet. Other characters have also lost their lives admist the family feuds. The Friar could be considered to be one of the reasons for the downfall of Romeo and Juliet's characters. Alternatively, the family feud between the montagues and the Capulets can be another reason for the tragic ending. Finally, the audience might think that fate had a huge role to play in the tragedy.

Shakespeare uses an array of themes, language and imagery in order to highlight different ideologies and messages circulating the ideas of love, family, rivalry and fate.

FATE   DEATH   FAMILY   LOVE   HONOUR   PEACE

THEMES, CONTEXT AND MOTIFS

THEMES

The forbidden love between Romeo and Juliet draws upon many themes. The key themes in *Romeo and Juliet* are outlined below. Note how all these themes interlink with other themes, which solidifies the structure and narrative of the play.

Love Vs. Hate

Shakespeare deals with the concept of love throughout the play. The meaning, causes and impact surrounding love are all explored in *Romeo and Juliet*, and Shakespeare does this successfully through his use of language, style and imagery.

The developing relationship between Romeo and Juliet is seen right from the offset, and the audience see how their relationship impacts on all the other characters in the play.

The best way to get a good idea about the concept of love and how, where and why it appears in the play is through examples. Below we have provided you a table outlining some of the key features about love, allowing you to fill in some of the table as you read the text.

Example	Type of Love	Evidence	Meaning/Effect
Romeo meets Juliet for the first time	Love at first sight	"For I ne'er saw true beauty until tonight"	It's powerful, exciting and demonstrates the idea of young love
Juliet is only thirteen	Young love	"She's way to young to be a bride"	Juliet is represented as headstrong and passionate
	True love		

Example	Type of Love	Evidence	Meaning/Effect
	Courtly love		
	Sexual love		
	Puppy love		
	Traditional love		
	Friendly love		

Key quotations to consider:

- *"Thus with a kiss I die"*
- *"Don't waste your love on somebody, who doesn't value it"*
- *"You kiss by the book"*
- *"What's in a name? that which we call a rose / By any other name*

> *would smell as sweet."*

- *"Under loves heavy burden do I sink"*

- *"My only love sprung from my only hate"*

- *"You are a lover. Borrow Cupid's wings and soar with them above a common bound"*

- *"Leap to these arms"*

- *"My naked weapon"*

- *"Thy love did read by rote that could not spell"*

- *"Eyes, look your last! / Arms, take your last embrace!"*

- *"Here's much to do with hate, but more with love"*

On the other hand, Shakespeare also uses hate as a way to counteract the idea of love. The hatred between the Montagues and the Capulets is presented right from the offset in the Prologue. The use of the words "mutiny", "rage" and "strife" reinforce this idea of hatred.

Family Relationships

In the Prologue, the Chorus instantly draws on family and conflict. Here, the audience are introduced to "two households" – the Montagues and the Capulets. Although they are "both alike in dignity", in other words, have the same social standing, we are told that we are going to witness a messy family feud between the two families.

Shakespeare portrays family relationships as being strained and distant. Despite coming from high social standings, both Romeo and Juliet are characters that come from a family that is far from loving and familial.

There are many family relationships represented throughout the play. The idea of family loyalty, relationships, honour and duty are all key ideas that you should consider in relation to different family relationships.

Example	Evidence	Meaning/Effect
Juliet's relationship with Tybalt	"[They fight, and Romeo kills Tybalt]"	Despite Romeo killing her cousin, Juliet remains by her husband's side. This shows how little her relationship to her cousin means to her.
Juliet's relationshp with the Nurse	"Thou wast the prettiest babe that ere I nursed"	This shows their relationship to be close, implying the idea of being like family
Juliet's relationship with her mother		
Juliet's relationship with her father		
Romeo's relationship with the Friar		
Romeo's relationship with Rosaline		
Romeo's relationship with his parents		
Romeo's relationship with with Tybalt		

Key quotations to consider:

* *"Two households, both alike in dignity"*

* *"Deny thy father and refuse thy name"*

- *"Tybalt, the reason that I have to love thee doth much excuse the appertaining rage"*

- *"Shall I speak ill of him that is my husband?"*

- *"We have a curse in having her"*

- *"Hang thee, young baggage, disobedient wretch"*

- *"Too soon marred are those so early made"*

- *"Henceforward I am ever ruled by you"*

Fate

Right from the offset, the audience are made aware of Romeo and Juliet's fate. Often in the play, Shakespeare suggests that we cannot always control our lives, and instead it's left to this idea of fate.

In the opening Prologue, the Chorus represent the characters of Romeo and Juliet as being "star-cross'd lovers" implying that their relationship is doomed.

The audience are always made aware about the fate of the protagonists. Talk about death, graves, curses and continuous conflict highlights the dreaded fate of what's to come.

Example	Evidence	Meaning/Effect
The Prologue	"Star-cross'd lovers"	This reinforces that Romeo and Juliet's relationship is doomed from the beginning - and the play has not officially begun!
Romeo has a funny feeling about attending the ball	"Hanging in the stars"	Romeo fears that something is destined to happen if he attends the ball
Romeo sees Juliet and believes her to be dead		

Key quotations to consider:

- *"From forth the fatal loins of these two foes / A pair of star-cross'd lovers take their life"*

- *"O, I am fortune's fool"*

- *"My grave is like to by my wedding bed"*

- *"I could not send it - here it is again - [Returning the letter]"*

- *"Is it e'en so? - Then I defy you, stars!"*

- *"Ah, what an unkind hour / Is guilty of this lamentable chance!"*

Conflict

Conflict is without a doubt one of the play's most central themes. The two warring families – the Montagues and the Capulets have been taught to hate one another. Not only does this impact family members but other members of the city.

The theme of conflict also ties in to other themes such as honour, feuds, power and control. Conflict is seen numerous times, and shown through:

- The two families – the Capulets and the Montagues;

- The inner conflict when Romeo finds out that Juliet is a Capulet, and vise versa;

- The conflict between Juliet and her father;

- The conflict between Romeo and Tybalt.

The characters in the play possess a strong sense of honour. The characters are easily drawn into fights in order to defend their family honour.

The violence and conflict gets progressively worse as the play comes to a dramatic ending. The only way that you can escape the feud appears to be death – take Romeo, Juliet, Tybalt and Mercutio for example.

Example	Evidence	Meaning/Effect
The Montagues and the Capulets	"Two households both alike in dignity...where civil blood makes civil hands unclean"	This reinforces an ancient grudge that the two familes have with one another. This is part of their daily lives.
Juliet's inner conflict	"That I must love a loathed enemy"	This signifies how Juliet is unable to change her feelings towards Romeo, despite their families being at each other's throats
Romeo's inner conflict		
Tybalt Vs. Romeo		

Key quotations to consider:

- *"Deny thy father and refuse thy name"*

- *"Either thou or I, or both, must go with him"*

- *"My only love sprung from my only hate"*

- *"These violent delights have violent ends"*

- *"His name is Romeo, and a Montague; the only son of your great enemy"*

- *"Romeo...thou art a villain"*

- *"Tybalt, you ratcatcher, will you walk?"*

Nature

The theme of nature is also apparent throughout *Romeo and Juliet*. Throughout the play, the use of nature and plant imagery are used to convey the idea of love. The way that the flowers grow and define a world of beauty resembles the beauty and love between Romeo and Juliet.

There are lots of characters who make reference to plants and/ or nature. Below we have included a table, again giving a couple of examples of nature quotes based on who said them and the effect.

Character	Evidence	Meaning/Effect
Romeo	"That which we call a rose by any other word would smell as sweet"	Romeo believes that his name does not define who he is. He won't stop loving Juliet because of the family feuds.
Juliet	"This bud of love, by summer's ripening breath"	Juliet uses flower imagery to show the quick progression in hers and Romeo's relationship. It suggests that overtime, their relationship will continue to grow
The Nurse		
Lady Capulet		

Key quotations to consider:

• *"Wither" and "ripe"*

• *"And I will make thy swan a crow"*

• *"Verona's summer hath not such a flower"*

- *"So shows a snowy dove trooping with crows"*

- *"That which we call a rose by any other word would smell as sweet"*

- *"Summer's ripening breath, may prove a beauteous flower when we next meet"*

- *"My bounty is as boundless as the sea; my love as deep: the more I give to thee the more I have, for both are infinite"*

- *"Sweet flower, with flowers thy bridal bed I strew"*

CONTEXT

In order to put *Romeo and Juliet* into perspective, you will need to have a good understanding about William Shakespeare, the origins, influence, and social and historical backgrounds underlying the text.

The Setting

It is often believed that the play is based on a true story. Supposedly, it's based loosely on an Italian love story set in 3rd Century.

Shakespeare wrote his version of the tale in 1594, based on Arthur Brooke's poem in 1562.

The setting of *Romeo and Juliet* was written in the Elizabethan Era (also known as the Renaissance). This time period focussed heavily on religion, politics, science, arts and language.

As mentioned in one of the opening chapters, *Romeo and Juliet* is set in the Italian city of Verona.

Example	Evidence	Meaning/Effect
Verona	"In fair Verona, where we lay our scene"	The story takes place in Verona, Italy. This is where the bulk of the action takes place.

Religion and Catholicism

At the time of writing, religion played a huge part in daily life. *Romeo and Juliet* references religious concepts throughout the play.

There are a few key facts that you should make yourself aware of regarding religion and historical context:

*   *Romeo and Juliet* was set in a Catholic society. This society has a strong belief in damnation as a result of moral sin. Examples of moral sins in the time in which this Shakespearean text was written included bigamy and suicide.

*   At the time this was written, 'The Reformation' had just occured. England broke free from Henry VIII's papal control and instead became a protestant society.

*   After this, society became more relaxed and open, and less oppressive.

In terms of religion, the Church played a huge role in both society and *Romeo and Juliet*.

THE CHURCH

In Shakespearean times, the Church played a significant role in everybody's life. It was custom for everyone to attend Church on Sunday. Anyone who didn't attend was punished with a fine.

Shakespeare uses lots of religious imagery throughout *Romeo and Juliet*.

Example	Evidence	Meaning/Effect
Juliet speaks to Romeo	"Which is the god of my idolatry"	Juliet swears her love for Romeo by saying that Romeo is her god. Shakespeare could be showing how worshipping one god might be dangerous
Romeo speaks to Juliet	"Call be but love and I'll be new baptized"	This references him being baptized in a church. He would give up his identity of being Romeo

Gender

When we speak about gender, it is apparent that there are clear distinctions between the male and female charactes.

Take a look at some of the key ideas surrounding the theme of gender. Can you spot any examples as you read through *Romeo and Juliet*?

• Women were seen to have less power than men. Female charactes were seen to have to obey men and do what they were told.

• A woman's main role in society in Elizabethan times was to satisfy the man, no matter what.

• This is also true with regards to daughters. Daughters were considered to be disobedient if they did not obey their fathers.

Example	Evidence	Meaning/Effect
Juliet disobeys her fathers orders to marry Paris	"Graze where you will you shall not house with me"	This reinforces how women are often seen to be oppressed by men. The fact that she disobeys her father suggests that she is 'garbage'
Lord Capulet gives orders to his wife	"Give me my long sword, ho!"	This shows how the male characters have great dominance over the females

Family and Marriage

Shakespeare's plays often drew upon conflict in relation to parent and child relationships. This is obvious throughout *Romeo and Juliet*, especially through the characters of Juliet and her father.

Below we have outlined a few key points that you should remember about family:

• The father of each household was considered as the undisputed head. In the 21st century, the idea of a male bread-winner has slightly changed, and females now play a more active role.

• In Elizabethan times, women had no rights or authority with regards to the law. They were unable to own property or money.

- Children were subject to being 'property' of male figures. Whether this was for their father or their partner, they had little say in what happened to them.

- At the time in which the play was set, it was not uncommon for young females to be married at an early age, sometimes as early at thirteen!

- Children were often raised by a nurse and had little interaction with their parents.

Example	Evidence	Meaning/Effect
Juliet is willing to give up her identity	"And I'll no longer be a Capulet"	The fact that she is willing to give up her identity to be with Romeo shows her love for him despite being a Montague
Juliet knows how influential her parents are	"I'll look to like, looking liking move; / But no more deep will I endart mine eye"	Juliet is saying that although she will follow her mother's advice by thinking about Paris, she is doubtful as to whether her feelings will change towards him

In this time, men and women were only able to get married in church. Traditionally, men and women were only able to live together if they were married.

- *Romeo and Juliet* is set in a religious society.

- The only way the two characters can be together is through marriage. That means Romeo and Juliet were subject to religion right from the offset.

- The audience witnesses Juliet marry Romeo. So, when it comes to her marrying Paris, this would be against the law of the Church.

- Another religious theme which is apparent in the play is sin. Romeo and Juliet commit a sin by committing suicide.

- The Friar is a religious figure in the play, which emphasizes how key this theme is to the narrative.

Audience

William Shakespeare's works appealed to the majority. Just like today, ticket prices were based on whereabouts you sat.

Shakespeare wanted to target a mass audience, from merchants and nobles, to poorer people.

When it comes to reading the works of Shakespeare, it is important that, as the reader, you are able to understand how Shakespeare appealed to his audience.

In his works, Shakespeare used language, imagery, themes, characters and narrative to appeal to his targeted audience. We will look at each of the aforementioned in more detail.

MOTIFS

In narratives, motifs act as symbolic reference which helps to enhance different themes and feelings.

Romeo and Juliet uses several motifs (or symbols) in order to create different emotions and effects.

Celestial Imagery

Celestial imagery is used to invigorate the five senses and compare things in a celestial way.

Stars and heaven are often referenced in *Romeo and Juliet*. Shakespeare did this to create particular meaning and effect for Elizabethan audiences.

Example	Evidence	Meaning/Effect
The Prologue	"A pair of star cross'd lovers"	Star crossed lovers implies that their fates have already been chosen, and that fate has a tragic ending

Example	Evidence	Meaning/Effect
Romeo is thinking of attending the Capulet's party	"I fear too early, for my mind misgives / Some consequences yet hanging in the stars"	Stars are referenced to symbolise Romeo's destiny. He knows that attending the Capulet's party could have major consequences
Juliet speaks to Romeo	"O, swear not by the moon, th' inconstant moon"	Juliet uses celestial imagery to tell Romeo that he needs to be sure that his love for her is true. His love cannot be changing like the phases on a moon

Light vs. Dark

One of the most apparent motifs running throughout *Romeo and Juliet* involves the interplay of light vs dark. This is often referred to with regards to imagery of day and night.

Although light (day) is not always good, and dark (night) is not always bad, this allows the audience to gain a sense of contrast, and hints at oppositions.

A great example of the light and dark motif is the balcony scene. The sun and the moon are discussed in great lengths which emphasises the transformation between day and night. Shakespeare could be doing this to explore the transformation in Romeo and Juliet's relationship.

Example	Evidence	Meaning/Effect
Romeo talks to Juliet	"the torches to burn bright"	Shakespeare is using light imagery to show how Juliet has brightened up Romeo's life by referencing to light
The morning after Romeo and Juliet spend the night together	"More light and light: more dark and dark our woes"	This indicates that Romeo and Juliet must part before the light arrives to ensure that Romeo isn't killed. Darkness is a great way to imply this tragic ending

Poison

Both sleep inducing and lethal, poison is used in the final Act which results in the deaths of both Romeo and Juliet. Technically, Juliet did not die from the poison, she stabbed herself, but that would never have occurred if it wasn't for the sleeping potion.

The poison symbolizes the feud between the Capulet family and the Montague family. The feud seen between the two families is deadly, much like poison in its most literal sense.

Poison is the catalyst for Romeo and Juliet's double suicide. This tragic ending marks the end of not only the love between Romeo and Juliet, but also the end of the family feud.

Example	Evidence	Meaning/Effect
Juliet uses a sleep inducing potion	"Romeo, Romeo, Romeo! Here's drink. I drink to thee"	Juliet uses a sleep inducing potion in the hopes of Romeo waking her and running away together. This clearly highlights the love she has for him
Romeo drinks a lethal potion	"Here's to my love! O true apothecary, Thy drugs are quick. Thus with a kiss I die."	When Romeo believes that Juliet is dead, he still wants to be with her, even if that results in his own death. Again, this shows the love and tragedy of Romeo and Juliet's fate and destiny

Time

Time is another major topic that can be discussed in relation to *Romeo and Juliet*. Even the Chorus makes reference to time by stating that the play will last for 2 hours.

Time plays a role in the narrative. Romeo and Juliet's relationship escalates very quickly. This suggests that both Romeo and Juliet are impatient people. For them, time is going extremely quickly, and they are anxious to make the most of the time they have left. It is a whirlwind romance, in many respects.

Example	Evidence	Meaning/Effect
Romeo speaks to Juliet	"sad hours seem long"	This implies that they feel like time is dragging, and they wish for it to move quicker in order to be together sooner
Juliet speaks to Romeo	"Tomorrow! Tis twenty year till then"	Again, this quotation demonstrates how time to them appears to be moving slowly

LITERARY TECHNIQUES

William Shakespeare uses an array of literary techniques in order to enhance his writing and create further meaning.

In this chapter, we will take a look at some of the most key techniques used in *Romeo and Juliet*.

Reading vs. Watching

One of the most important things to remember when reading *Romeo and Juliet* is that it is still a play. *Romeo and Juliet* was written with the sole intention of being performed. Shakespeare had to make sure that the stagecraft behind the play was effective and entertaining.

The importance of stagecraft:

- Stagecraft is the ability to write something that can be performed on a stage.

- In Shakespearean times, the theatre was the biggest forms of entertainment. That means watching shows was popular amongst all types of people.

- The stagecraft in Elizabethan plays is very different to how plays are performed in the 21st century. They were limited with regards to backdrops, scene settings and props. Thus, the script is the ultimate resource to creating a successful play.

- *Romeo and Juliet* was intended to be moving, romantic and dramatic.

Puns

Romeo and Juliet uses lots of wordplays and puns. This was a common writing technique at the time Shakespeare wrote this play. Audiences enjoyed puns – whether they were funny or simply clever wordplays, they were a great way to lighten the mood.

Puns are notorious techniques in the works of Shakespeare. They are often used to amuse the audience and help keep the audience laughing and lighten the scene, even in a tragedy.

Read through the play and find examples of puns and/or wordplays. Write them down in the table below and explain why you think

Shakespeare has used this pun. What effect would this have on an audience? We have provided an example to get you started.

Puns	Explanation
"Ask for me tomorrow, and you shall find me a grave man"	Mercutio's pun when he is dying emphasises not only how serious his injuries are, but also the fact that he is going to be buried in his "grave" tomorrow. Shakespeare uses this pun to try and lighten the mood on an event that is actually quite sad

Foreshadowing and Metaphors

Shakespeare also uses foreshadowing and metaphors to give hints about what will happen later on in the play. This helps to bring life to his play and allow the audience to fully engage with the goings-on.

Foreshadowing and Metaphors	Explanation
"Life were better ended by thy hate, than death prorogued, wanting of the love"	This suggests that Romeo would much rather have Juliet's love and die, as opposed to not have her love and die anyway. This foreshadows Romeo's death, lying next to his love, Juliet

Foreshadowing and Metaphors	Explanation

Paradox

A paradox is a statement that appears to contradict itself, but actually holds some truth behind it.

Paradox	Explanation
"My only love sprung from my only hate"	This statement seems to contradict itself because love and hate are opposites. However, realistically Juliet and Romeo are from two rivalling families, and therefore their love has begun despite the hatred that remains between their parents

Soliloquy

Shakespeare is a master of placing soliloquies in his work. Soliloqueys are a speech that an actor gives as though they are talking to themselves.

Soliloquy	Explanation
"But soft, what light through yonder window breaks..."	Romeo's soliloquy talks about his affection for Juliet. This allows the audience to gain a sense of how he is truly feeling

Personification

Personification is a great way to describe an inanimate thing as if it were a person.

Personification	Explanation
""Now old desire does in his deathbed lie, / And young afection gapes to be his heir"	The words "old desire" suggests Rosaline to be a dying out thought of Romeo's. "Young affection" suggests that Romeo's love is new and passionate

Similes

Imagery is when things are described in a vivid and descriptive way. Similes offer the chance to do exactly that. Similes can be used to describe one thing like something else.

Similes	Explanation
"Too rude, too boisterous, and it pricks like thorn"	This suggests how a character's personality is being compared to a "thorn". This suggests that they are sharp, cruel and strong

Dramatic Irony

Shakespeare also takes advantage of dramatic irony. Dramatic irony in it's most basic sense involves an outcome that you were not expecting.

The tale of *Romeo and Juliet* uses irony throughout the play.

Dramatic Irony	Explanation
"From forth the fatal loins of these two foes / A pair of star-cross'd lovers take their life, / Whose misadventured piteous overthrows, / Do with their death bury their parent's strife"	The death of these characters eventually leads to the end in the feud between their families

Finding Literary Techniques

Now that we have provided you with a few examples of different literary techniques, we are now going to provide you some space to find as many technique examples as you can. When doing so, think about why Shakespeare has used this. What effect does this have on an audience?

Literary Technique	Evidence	Meaning/Effect
Oxymoron		
Pun		
Antithesis		

Literary Technique	Evidence	Meaning/Effect
Simile		
Metaphor		
Personifica-tion		
Irony		

Literary Technique	Evidence	Meaning/Effect
Foreshadow		
Soliloquy		
Allusion		
Hyperbole		

Literary Technique	Evidence	Meaning/Effect
Alliteration		
Figurative Language		
Rhyming		
Poetic Devices		

POETRY IN SHAKESPEARE

SHAKESPEARE AND HIS POEMS

Aside from his literary genius in creating plays, William Shakespeare also spent a great deal of his writing career producing poems.

In total, Shakespeare wrote 154 sonnets, and five long narrative poems. His long narrative poems are less well-known, and he is mostly famous for his exceptional play writing skills and love poems.

When reading through *Romeo and Juliet*, see if you can spot any poetic techniques that Shakespeare is renowned for.

SONNETS

Shakespeare wrote 154 sonnets, each numbered (1-154).

Traditionally, a sonnet is a 14 line poem which is written in iambic pentameter. Shakespeare almost always used iambic pentameter when writing his sonnets.

What is Iambic Pentameter?

*   Ten syllables to each line;
*   Five pairs of unstressed and stressed syllables (alternating).

    (Da dum, / da dum, / da dum, / da dum, / da dum)

Sometimes Shakespeare would break free from this, in order to add extra colour and feeling to his poetry.

RHYMING PATTERNS

The rhyming pattern of English sonnets is as follows:

a b a b ⟶ Lines 1 and 3 rhyme / lines 2 and 4 rhyme

c d c d ⟶ Lines 5 and 7 rhyme / lines 6 and 8 rhyme

e f e f ⟶ Lines 9 and 11 rhyme / lines 10 and 12 rhyme

g g ⟶ Lines 13 and 14 rhyme

We have provided an example using Shakespeare's Sonnet 29, to emphasise the rhyming pattern:

SONNET 29

When in disgrace with Fortune and men's <u>eyes</u>,	*A*
I all alone beweep my outcast <u>state</u>,	*B*
And trouble deaf heaven with my bootless <u>cries</u>,	*A*
And look upon myself and curse my <u>fate</u>,	*B*
Wishing me like to one more rich in <u>hope</u>,	*C*
Featured like him, like him with friends <u>possessed</u>,	*D*
Desiring this man's art and that man's <u>scope</u>,	*C*
With what I most enjoy contented <u>least</u>,	*D*
Yet in these thoughts my self almost <u>despising</u>,	*E*
Haply I think on thee, and then my <u>state</u>,	*F*
(Like to the lark at break of day <u>arising</u>	*E*
From sullen earth) sings hymns at heaven's <u>gate</u>,	*F*
For thy sweet love remembered such wealth <u>brings</u>,	*G*
That then I scorn to change my state with <u>kings</u>.	*G*

Rhythm is a key technique used in poetry, in order to create emotions, mood and atmosphere.

Sonnets in particular use a beat to keep the momentum and flow of the narrative. For example, poems about love would have an upbeat, positive rhythm, whereas something more serious would have a very different beat.

ANALYSING SONNETS

The first 126 sonnets in Shakespeare's collection appear to address a man. These sonnets deal with themes including love, nobility, music, time and betrayal.

Sonnets 127 to 152 appear to address a woman. The themes in language in these poems seem much more personal and intense compared to the first 126 sonnets.

The last two sonnets seem trivial. They appear to be written in a style to that of Greek epigrams. Although these poems do touch upon the relationship between Shakespeare and the woman (in sonnets 127 to 152), these two poems take a different turn in terms of language and narration.

When analysing sonnets, you should consider the following things:

- Narration;
- Tone of voice;
- 1st person or 3rd person;
- Imagery;
- Themes;
- Rhythm;
- Mood;
- Feelings;
- Structure;
- Context.

POETRY TECHNIQUES IN HIS PLAYS

Shakespeare often used poetic devices in his plays. He did this on purpose and it proved really effective in theatre performances.

Most of Shakespeare's plays were written using iambic pentameter. He used this technique for the dialogue of higher-class characters. For lower-class characters, they would speak in prose as opposed to verses.

This would differentiate the social standings between different characters.

Poetry

PREPARATION FOR EXAMS

HOW TO PREPARE

The first step to success at English GCSE is to know what you're talking about. Make sure you read the play carefully. If it helps, find film adaptations which are faithful to the original material – this can help you visualise the events of the novel or play more easily.

On top of this, there are plenty of websites and books which offer interpretations and critiques of the texts that you're studying. You can use these as a guide to the text, or as arguments in your essays.

For plays, you should try to remember the key events which take place, as well as the main characters and their personalities. Creating a small fact file with profiles for each character can be a fun way of summarising them and their role in the text. If it helps, you can even use descriptions of the characters' looks to sketch them, giving you a broader picture of what they would be like.

For the story, try to reduce the book into the key events. Preferably, try to find the three key events of the text – the ones which define its three acts. Then, reduce these three chunks into three smaller events, meaning that you have nine events which drive the plot of the novel or play. You can then sort these events into a flowchart so that you can easily remember the order of events.

Romeo and Juliet meet	Romeo and Juliet plan to run away together	Romeo and Juliet die

From here, the nine key events could be:

1. Romeo and Juliet attend the ball.
2. Romeo and Juliet meet.
3. The balcony scene occurs.

4. Romeo meets with Friar Lawrence to make wedding arrangements.
5. Lord Capulet arranges for Juliet to marry Paris.
6. Romeo kills Tybalt and is banished.
7. Juliet takes the drug to feign her death.
8. Romeo drinks the poison upon finding Juliet 'dead' in her tomb.
9. Juliet awakens to find Romeo's body, then takes her own life.

Finally, you will need to remember the core themes for the play. Generally, the texts you study will have one or two primary themes (in the case of *Romeo and Juliet*, these might be 'love' and 'fate'). In addition to this, there may be a few minor themes. Additional reading of secondary sources, such as literary criticism, will reveal some of these ideas. Experiment with different revision techniques which suit you in order to remember the key themes of the text, as well as key events, characters, or lines of the text which relate to them.

Sadly, English at GCSE often requires you to remember key quotes. This can be annoying, but the best way to learn them is to read them, write them or listen to them being spoken over and over until they stick in your head.

Preparation is key to securing top marks in your GCSE. The best way to prepare for your exam, is to undergo lots of sample test questions and mock exams. Equally important, you should understand how you will be assessed during the exam, including understanding the exam question.

UNDERSTANDING THE EXAM QUESTION

Within the Shakespeare section of your GCSE English exam, there are four main skills that you will need to demonstrate throughout your answers.

Below we have outlined these four main skills which you should consider when practising your exam questions:

1. Use appropriate and relevant examples and quotes from the text in order to back up your answers.

2. Explore the importance of language, form and structure, and how Shakespeare uses these in order to create meaning and effect.

3. Consider social, cultural and historical backgrounds and why this is important to the overall narrative.

4. Write in a clear, well-structured manner to ensure that you gain extra marks. Remember, 5% of your Literature marks will be given to correct grammar, punctuation and spelling. This refers to quotations as well. If you quote from the text, be sure to use the correct spelling and punctuation – you will be marked down otherwise!

One of the best ways to fully understand the question is to underline or highlight keywords in the question. This will allow you to focus on the key points of the question.

EXAMPLE

> How does Shakespeare present the theme of love in the play?
>
> Refer to the following extract in your answer.

We can break down this question by underlining key points of the question. This will allow us to work out what needs to be discussed in our answer...

> How does Shakespeare present the theme of love in the play?
>
> Refer to the following extract in your answer.

• Questions asking 'how' want you to think about the writer's techniques.

• The underlined word 'present' wants you to discuss structure, form and language.

• The key theme is love. This is what needs to be discussed.

• You need to refer to the extract provided to you.

When it comes to exam questions, you need to understand what the question is ACTUALLY asking you.

Below we have broken down a few ways in which questions can be asked to you, and what this means for you and your writing.

Wording of question	What you need to do...
How does...	These type of questions want you to analyse the literary techniques used. How does the author get their points across? What evidence can you find to support this?
Explain / Explore...	These type of questions want you to talk about a particular character, idea or theme. Again, you should use literary techniques to support your claims.
Give examples...	These type of questions are asking you to use direct quotations from the text. You need to describe the quotes using your own words and opinions.
Refer to...	These type of questions want you to refer to a particular extract or the whole play (whatever is stated). Marks will be lost if you do not refer to what is being asked in the question.

READ THE QUESTION CAREFULLY

Particularly for exams, people tend to rush through their answers, scared that they are going to run out of time. When they do this, they fail to read what is actually being asked of them.

Consider the following before writing your response:

- *What is the question asking you to do?*

- *Is the question asking more than one thing?*

- *How do you need to structure your response?*

- *What kind of style should your writing use?*

- *What kind of language should you use in your response?*

Reading the question carefully will ensure that you respond to what is being asked.

THE IMPORTANCE OF PLANNING

Good planning and timing are two of the most important skills that you can learn and practise before sitting your exam. In fact, being able to plan effectively and get your timing down will serve you well in almost every career, so it pays to put the effort in now.

Before you go into your exam, you should find out exactly what the structure of the exam will be. Try and find out the answers to the following questions:

*   How long do I have for the whole exam?

*   What type of questions will be asked (essay, single-word answers, short paragraph, problem solving)?

*   How many marks are there in the whole exam?

*   Roughly, how many marks are available per question?

*   If applicable, how much time is there for planning?

Once you have this information, you can get to work on applying this to your revision schedule. For example, when you attempt a mock exam, you should try to make the situation as close to the real thing as possible. You should plan and time your mock exam as if it were an actual exam.

Don't dive straight in!

The most important thing to remember when it comes to writing, is to take your time and PLAN what you are going to say.

Examiners will know if you have structured your response thoroughly, or just dived head first and written off the top of your head.

Planning is a crucial step for any good writer. There is no wrong or right way to plan; you just need to find a way that you feel comfortable with.

Taking notes from written text

If you are making notes from a piece of text, you should consider the following:

1. Keep your notes simple!

- Try not to ramble on.
- Keep your notes on point, focused and short.
- The snappier your notes are, the easier they are to remember.
- Think of keywords and phrases.

2. Know what you want to say!

- Before you begin writing, you will need to know ROUGHLY what it is you want to say.
- What main points do you want to cover?
- What is the purpose of the text?
- Who is going to be reading the text?
- Consider what you want to achieve from your written text.

3. Using spider diagrams

- Spider diagrams help you to keep your notes all on one page.
- At a glance, you are able to clearly see all of your main points/ideas.
- They group points together, which you can then extend even further.

4. Using linear notes

- This is a more detailed way of making notes.
- Your notes will be separated with the use of headings and sub-headings.
- Underline key words and phrases in each section.
- Use abbreviations to shorten your notes down.
- Leave space to add more detail if necessary.
- Bullet points and numbering are great to use under each sub-

heading.

Structuring your notes

When it comes to planning, especially for stories, you want to make sure to draft some key points on a few areas:

CHARACTERS

Wizard   Dragon

Knight   Devil

THEMES

NARRATIVE

SETTING

BEGINNING, MIDDLE AND END

Essays are a great way to structure your writing.

Essays are a form of writing which allow you to answer a question.

What all good essays need

All good essays need a clear and focused structure. You can achieve this by creating an introduction, a middle and an end.

INTRODUCTION

- Outline what direction your essay is going to take.
- You could include a hypothesis.
- Use keywords from the question.
- 2-3 sentences is sufficient for an introduction.
- The reader should be able to read your introduction and conclusion, and know what your essay is about.

MAIN BODY

- Answer the question by making 3-4 points.
- Support these points with examples, quotes and analysis.
- Make sure you keep referring to the question.
- 3-4 paragraphs is sufficient for an essay.
- Analyse and explain key points, their relevance and your opinions.

CONCLUSION

- Summarise the key points you've made and how they are important/relevant.
- DO NOT introduce any new points in the conclusion.
- Make sure you write a sentence referring to the question.
- The reader should be able to read your introduction and conclusion, and know what your essay is about.

On the next few pages, we have created a template which you can use and redraw to help you when it comes to structuring your essays. I've also provided a sample essay, and highlighted key points throughout the essay.

As well as structure, essays also need to flow, use effective language, use the correct tone, and of course, answer the question.

ESSAY FEATURES	EXPLANATION
Language	Consider what language is best. For essays, formal and technical language is great. Use long fancy words only if you know the meaning of them.
Tone and style	You need to set the tone. Is it a serious or light-hearted essay? Your language should reflect this.
Paragraphing	Use a paragraph for each new point. Your introduction and conclusion will form paragraphs, and then you'll have 3 or 4 paragraphs for your main body.
Literary techniques	Avoid repetition. Rhetorical questions are great to interact your reader. Consider what techniques you can use to enhance your writing (metaphors, personification etc.)

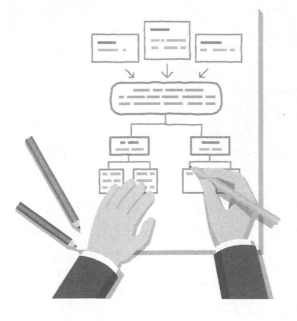

Key words and phrases

For each section of your essay, we have provided some key words and phrases.

INTRODUCTORY WORDS

In this essay

We are introduced to

Within this essay

I am going to

OPINIONATED WORDS

I believe

I think

I am convinced

My opinion

My point of view

I feel

It seems that

TRANSITION WORDS

First/second/third

Consequently

Although

Equally important

In addition

Obviously

Furthermore

Additionally

CONCLUSION WORDS

In conclusion

Finally

In summary

Overall

We can see that

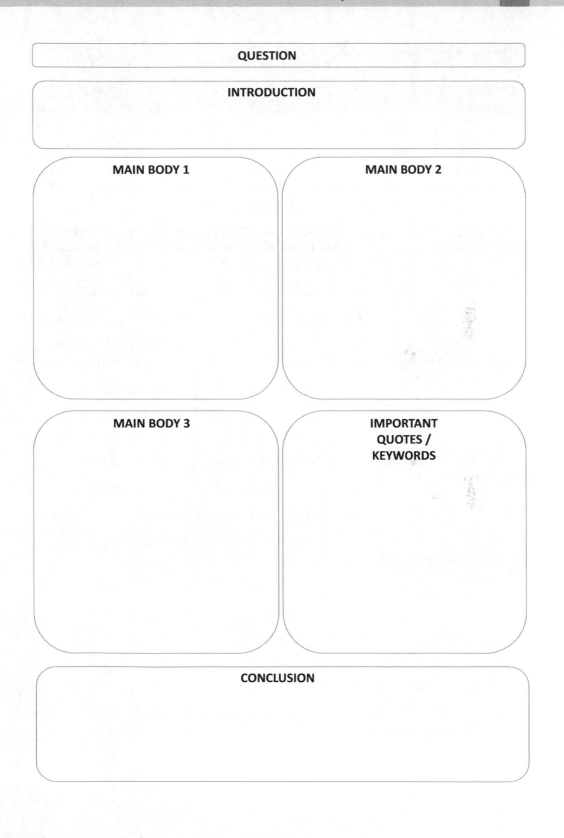

QUESTION

INTRODUCTION

MAIN BODY 1

MAIN BODY 2

MAIN BODY 3

IMPORTANT
QUOTES /
KEYWORDS

CONCLUSION

WHAT TO EXPECT

At GCSE, English is divided into two separate subjects – English Literature and English Language. Depending on your exam board, these questions may be worth between 50% and 60% of your overall English Literature or English Language GCSE:

	AQA	Edexcel
English Literature Paper 1	1 hour, 45 minutes 64 marks Worth 40% of English Literature GCSE	1 hour, 45 minutes 80 marks Worth 50% of English Literature GCSE
English Literature Paper 2	2 hours, 15 minutes 96 marks Worth 60% of English Literature GCSE	2 hours, 15 minutes 80 marks Worth 50% of English Literature GCSE
English Language Paper 1	1 hour, 45 minutes 80 marks Worth 50% of English Language GCSE	1 hour, 45 minutes 64 marks Worth 40% of English Language GCSE
English Language Paper 2	1 hour, 45 minutes 80 marks Worth 50% of English Language GCSE	2 hours 96 marks Worth 60% of English Language GCSE

As you can see, marks are weighted slightly differently, depending on which exam board your course is on.

With regards to Shakespeare, this will appear in the Literature section of your English GCSE.

SHAKESPEARE EXAM QUESTIONS

This extract is taken from **Act II Scene II**. Romeo sees Juliet for the first time.

> **ROMEO**
>
> If I profane with my unworthiest hand
>
> This holy shrine, the gentle sin is this:
>
> My lips, two blushing pilgrims, ready stand
>
> To smooth that rough touch with a tender kiss.
>
> **JULIET**
>
> Good pilgrim, you do wrong your hand too much,
>
> Which mannerly devotion shows in this;
>
> For saints have hands that pilgrims' hands do touch,
>
> And palm to palm is holy palmers' kiss.
>
> **ROMEO**
>
> Have not saints lips, and holy palmers too?
>
> **JULIET**
>
> Ay, pilgrim, lips that they must use in prayer.

Question 1

Using examples from **Act II Scene II**, how does Shakespeare explore the relationship between Romeo and Juliet?

Write about:

- How Shakespeare presents Romeo in this extract;

- How Shakespeare conveys Romeo and Juliet's relationship in the overall play.

This extract is taken from **Act II Scene II**. Romeo declares his love for Juliet. (The balcony scene).

ROMEO

He jests at scars that never felt a wound.

   Juliet appears above at a window.

But, soft! what light through yonder window breaks?

It is the east, and Juliet is the sun.

Arise, fair sun, and kill the envious moon,

Who is already sick and pale with grief,

That thou her maid art far more fair than she:

Be not her maid, since she is envious;

Her vestal livery is but sick and green

And none but fools do wear it; cast it off.

It is my lady, O, it is my love!

O, that she knew she were!

She speaks yet she says nothing: what of that?

Her eye discourses; I will answer it.

I am too bold; 'tis not to me she speaks:

Two of the fairest stars in all the heaven,

Having some business, do entreat her eyes

To twinkle in their spheres till they return.

What if her eyes were there, they in her head?

The brightness of her cheek would shame those stars,

As daylight doth a lamp; her eyes in heaven

Would through the airy region stream so bright,

That birds would sing and think it were not night.

Question 2

Shakespeare contrasts day with night. What do you think this means in terms of Romeo and Juliet's relationship?

Write about:

* How Shakespeare uses language to convey meaning;

* How Shakespeare conveys Romeo and Juliet's relationship.

This extract is taken from **Act V Scene III**. Romeo and Juliet die.

JULIET

Go, get thee hence, for I will not away.

   Exit Friar Lawrence

What's here? a cup, closed in my true love's hand?

Poison, I see, hath been his timeless end:

O churl! drunk all, and left no friendly drop

To help me after? I will kiss thy lips;

Haply some poison yet doth hang on them,

To make me die with a restorative.

   Kisses Romeo.

Thy lips are warm.

   Enter Watchmen and Paris's Page

CHIEF WATCHMAN

   (To Page) Lead, boy: which way?

JULIET

Yea, noise? then I'll be brief. O happy dagger!

   Snatching Romeo's dagger

This is thy sheath; there rust, and let me die.

   (Stabs herself with Romeo's dagger and dies).

Question 3

Poison plays a literal and symbolic role in the play of *Romeo and Juliet*. Romeo drinks the potion after thinking his true love is dead. Juliet's death is a consequence of the poison. Explain how the poison acts as a symbol within the narrative.

Write about:

- How Shakespeare uses symbolism to create meaning;

- How Shakespeare explores Romeo and Juliet's relationship throughout the play.

Question 4

Using examples from *Romeo and Juliet*, how does Shakespeare explore how Romeo and Juliet's relationship is doomed from the beginning. Focus on language, imagery and themes.

Write about:

- How Shakespeare uses language and literary techniques to explore Romeo and Juliet's relationship and how it is doomed;

- The main themes and imagery explored throughout the play.

Question 5

In what way does Romeo and Juliet break free from traditional gender conventions? Use examples from the play to support your answer.

Write about:

- How Shakespeare uses language and imagery to create gender representations;

- The main themes, ideas and symbols used to signify that Shakespeare has broken free from traditional conventions.

Question 6

Discuss how Juliet's maturity levels change from the beginning of the play to the end of the play. Why does her maturity change? What affect does this have on the audience? Why is this important to the narrative?

Write about:

• How Shakespeare represents Juliet throughout the play, exploring any changes along the way;

• Why you think Shakespeare chooses to represent Juliet in this way.

Question 7

How does Juliet's relationship with her parents change throughout the course of the play?

Write about:

• Why Shakespeare represents this relationship in this way;

• What impact this would have on an audience.

Question 8

Describe Friar Lawrence's character.

Write about:

• How his character is significant to the overall play;

• What his relationship is like with other characters.

This extract is taken from **Act II Scene II**. Romeo declares his love for Juliet. (The balcony scene).

ROMEO

She speaks:

O, speak again, bright angel! for thou art

As glorious to this night, being o'er my head

As is a winged messenger of heaven

Unto the white-upturned wondering eyes

Of mortals that fall back to gaze on him

When he bestrides the lazy-pacing clouds

And sails upon the bosom of the air.

JULIET

O Romeo, Romeo! wherefore art thou Romeo?

Deny thy father, and refuse thy name;

Or, if thou wilt not, be but sworn my love,

And I'll no longer be a Capulet.

ROMEO

   [Aside] Shall I hear more, or shall I speak at this?

JULIET

'Tis but thy name that is my enemy;

Thou art thyself, though not a Montague.

What's Montague? it is not hand, nor foot,

Nor arm, nor face, nor any other part

Belonging to a man. O, be some other name!

What's in a name? that which we call a rose

By any other name would smell as sweet;

Question 9

Using examples from **Act II Scene II**, and other examples from *Romeo and Juliet*, how does Shakespeare explore celestial imagery?

Write about:

- How Shakespeare uses language and literary techniques to explore celestial imagery;

- Why Shakespeare does this and the impact this has on the audience.

Question 10

How does Shakespeare present different ideas of love?

Write about:

- Why Shakespeare explores different idea of love;

- Different characters and how they each represent love and what that brings to the play.

SUGGESTED COMMENTS

Question 1

- You can talk about the idea of coming-of-age romance.

- You can discuss how they are both willing to defy their parents and run away with one another – despite the family feuds between her family and his.

- Their love is conveyed in a strong, poetic way.

- Find different quotes and examples that use specific themes and imagery in order to convey this idea of romance.

- Romeo continues to express his love throughout the play.

- The pivotal scenes, the balcony scene and the death scene, highlight the strength of their love. The death scene in particular shows how they are willing to do anything (including killing themselves) in order to be with one another.

- You can talk about how Shakespeare explores this idea of classic romantic love.

QUOTATIONS TO CONSIDER:

"You kiss by th' book"

- This shows how Juliet teases Romeo for being very conventional in his ways of 'wooing' her.

"It is too rash, too unadvis'd, too sudden"

- Juliet realises how quickly their romance has escalated. Not only does this show naivety and innocence, but it also shows the strength of their love for one another.

"Did my heart love till now? Forswear it, sight! For I ne'er saw true beauty till this night."

- Romeo questions whether he's been in love before (with Rosaline), after seeing Juliet for the very first time.

"My lips, two blushing pilgrims, ready stand / To smooth that rough touch with a tender kiss"

- The language used in the dialogue between *Romeo and Juliet* is romantic, expressive, and poetic. This use of language clearly captures the romance between these two characters, which is probably why the play *Romeo and Juliet* can be classed as one of the all-time best love stories in literary history.

Question 2

- You can talk about how light and dark is constantly referenced throughout the play.

- Discuss how the light and dark does not always reflect the traditional idea of good vs. bad.

- The Balcony scene is a great example which offers lots of examples of light and dark imagery (sun and moon). Discuss why you think Shakespeare has done this.

- The darkness can be used to symbolize the tragic ending in Romeo and Juliet's relationship. This is a powerful technique which allows the audience to constantly be aware of how the play is going to end.

- The light and dark allows the audience to see Romeo and Juliet's relationship in many different ways. What ways are conveyed? Why do you think Shakespeare has done this?

QUOTATIONS TO CONSIDER:

"And Juliet is the sun"

- This reinforces how Romeo's life is lit up with Juliet in it. Juliet brightens up Romeo's life by comparing her to the sun - a bright and happy feeling.

"Two of the fairest stars in all the heaven"

- Again, heaven is used to symbolize light. This shows how Shakespeare is trying to represent Juliet in an angelic and beautiful way.

"O, swear not by the moon, the inconstant moon"

- The moon is used to contrast day with night. Shakespeare might have done this to show the transformation between day and night which could reflect the transformation in Romeo and Juliet's relationship. This also suggests the idea of time passing by.

Question 3

- The literal meaning of the poison is that it is the actual element that caused the death of Romeo.

- Symbolically, the poison acts as a visual aid for the destruction of Romeo and Juliet's relationship.

- The poison between their families as well as the poison (in literal terms), is a clear way of poisoning the love of Romeo and Juliet, which in the end results in their deaths.

QUOTATIONS TO CONSIDER:

"Romeo, Romeo, Romeo! Here's drink. I drink to thee"

- Juliet uses a sleep inducing potion in the hopes of Romeo waking her and running away together. This clearly highlights the love she has for him.

"Here's to my love! O true apothecary, Thy drugs are quick. Thus with a kiss I die."

- When Romeo believes that Juliet is dead, he still wants to be with her, even if that results in his own death. Again, this shows the love and tragedy of Romeo and Juliet's fate and destiny.

Question 4

- You can discuss how they are both willing to defy their parents and run away with one another – despite the family feuds between her family and his.

- The pivotal scenes, the balcony scene and the death scene, highlight the strength of their love. The death scene in particular shows how they are willing to do anything (including killing themselves) in order to be with one another.

- Discuss how the Prologue automatically states that the relationship between Romeo and Juliet is doomed. Why do you think Shakespeare does this so early on?

SUGGESTED COMMENTS

QUOTATIONS TO CONSIDER:

"If he be married, / My grave is likely to be my wedding bed"

- After seeing Romeo at the ball, Juliet's views towards love and marriage begin to change. As the audience/reader, we see how her maturity levels are beginning to change, and how she is changing from a young girl into a young woman.

"My unworthiest hand"

- The phrase "My unworthiest hand" implies that Romeo does not deem himself as being a worthy suitor for Juliet. The fact that his hand is unworthy foreshadows conflict between his family (the Montagues) and her family (the Capulets).

"Here's to my love! O true apothecary, Thy drugs are quick. Thus with a kiss I die."

- The literal meaning of the poison is that it is the actual element that caused the death of Romeo. Symbolically, the poison acts as a visual aid for the destruction of Romeo and Juliet's relationship. The poison between their families as well as the poison (in literal terms), is a clear way of poisoning the love of Romeo and Juliet, which in the end results in their deaths.

Question 5

- In Shakespearean times, men would be classed as the dominant figure who would use violence, aggression and manipulation in order to defeat their opponents.

- Women were often objects for men to win after a conquest. They played a dismissive role, and would be subject to the male figure in their lives.

- The character breaks free from traditional gender roles, by constantly being conveyed in a poetic manner.

- Romeo's masculinity is challenged throughout the play due to his feminine traits and language used. This is particularly true when it comes to his relationship with Juliet.

- Juliet is often conveyed as an independent, strong-minded woman.

- Although Romeo does defend his family, and does show signs of masculinity in terms of violence and aggression (the killing of Tybalt), as the male protagonist, he is still conveyed in a way that is not as masculine as other male protagonists in Shakespeare's works.

QUOTATIONS TO CONSIDER:

"Love is a smoke made with the fumes of sighs, / Being purg'd , a fire sparkling in lovers' eyes"

- This reinforces the poetic dialogue Romeo would use to express his feelings for Juliet. In terms of masculinity, this breaks free from traditional gender roles, as men would be viewed as figures who are strong and dominant – but the fact that Romeo expresses his views, shows his weakness (his love for Juliet) and therefore detracts from his masculinity.

"O, speak again, bright angel, for thou art / As glorious to this night, being o'er my head"

SUGGESTED COMMENTS

- This is a physical representation of women being more in control than men. The fact that Romeo is positioned lower than Juliet (Juliet is above in the window, whereas Romeo is standing on the ground outside), illustrates the change in gender roles.

"If that thy bent of love be honourable, / Thy purpose marriage, send me word to-morrow"

- Juliet breaks free from traditional female stereotypes. The fact that she is unmarried and quite forward in her dialogue reinforces her independence and strong-mindedness. At the time in which the play was written, this type of behaviour from women was deemed unacceptable and abnormal.

Question 6

- You should discuss how Juliet's character changes as the play progresses.

- At the beginning of the play, we view Juliet's character to be young, naïve, innocent and pure.

- As her love continues to blossom for Romeo, we see how Juliet's character becomes more developed.

- You need to explain why you think Shakespeare shows Juliet's maturity levels changing. Do you think it allows you to see transformations of age? Do you think Shakespeare wants you to relate to the changes that every person goes through from childhood to adolescence? Is there any other reasons why you think Shakespeare does this?

- Explain the impact this has on the audience. Showing the changes in maturity levels not only links back to theme of coming-of-age, but also creates quite a fast-paced rhythm for the overall narrative.

QUOTATIONS TO CONSIDER:

"It is an honour that I dream not of"

- When Juliet's mother asks her about her views on marriage (at the beginning of the play), Juliet's response highlights how she has not begun to think about love or marriage as of yet.

"If he be married, / My grave is likely to be my wedding bed"

- After seeing Romeo at the ball, Juliet's views towards love and marriage begin to change. As the audience/reader, we see how her maturity levels are beginning to change, and how she is changing from a young girl into a young woman.

"Shall I speak ill of him that is my husband? / As, poor my lord, what tongue shall smooth thy name / When I, thy three-hours' wife, have mangled it?"

- Here, we see Juliet recognising that love is not all plain-sailing. Instead, she starts to show understanding that difficulties and challenges lie ahead in marriage.

Question 7

- Juliet has a strained relationship with her mother. Juliet was raised by her Nurse, and therefore shows a lack of maternal affection from her mother.

SUGGESTED COMMENTS

- Her relationship is very traditional in terms of Elizabethan times. He is more concerned about marrying her off into a wealthy family as opposed to her actual happiness.

- Shakespeare portrays family relationships as being strained and distant. Despite coming from high social standings, both Romeo and Juliet are characters that come from a family that is far from loving and familial.

- There are many family relationships represented throughout the play. The idea of family loyalty, relationships, honour and duty are all key ideas that you should consider in relation to different family relationships.

QUOTATIONS TO CONSIDER:

"Hang thee, young baggage, disobedient wretch"

- This is the harsh response of Juliet's father when she refuses to marry Paris. This shows how traditions in Shakespearean times expect femlaes to obey the men. When Juliet disobeys, this leads to further conflict and tension within the play.

"I have done with thee"

- This is Juliet's mother's final line, which reinforces how obedience and loyalty play a huge role when focussing on family.

"And the continuance of their parent's rage"

- Again this signifies how Juliet's parents are often portrayed as angry and hostile.

Question 8

- Friar Lawrence is to that of a monk. The Friar hands out potions and plants which contain special powers.

- The Friar is a respected character.

- Explore whether or not the Friar plays a significant role in the downfall of Romeo and Juliet.

- Does the Friar's character change as the play progresses?

- Why do you think Shakespeare uses a 'friar' in the play *Romeo and Juliet*? What does this signify and what is its importance?

- The Friar is also represented as a wise character.

QUOTATIONS TO CONSIDER:

"O Lord, I could have stayed here all the night / To hear good counsel"

- Shakespeare brings in an element of religion and Catholicism by representing the Friar as a holy and respected character.

"Love moderately; long love doth so"

- The Friar often offers wise words to different characters throughout the play. This shows that he is a trusted character amongst the other people in the play.

"Young men's love then lies / Not truly in the hearts, but in their eyes"

- Friar Lawrence is saying that Romeo's character is fickle and suggests that Romeo has only fallen in love with Juliet because of her looks.

SUGGESTED COMMENTS

"These violent delights have violent ends"

- The Friar is suggesting that all good things come to an end. In this instance, the blossoming romance of Romeo and Juliet is struck down by the deaths of both characters. This highlights how impulsiveness and suddenness can have a tragic ending.

Question 9

- Celestial imagery is when references to heaven, stars and planets are made. The importance of celestial imagery is to invigorate the five sense and compare things to something in a celestial way.

- Stars and heaven are often referenced in *Romeo and Juliet*. Shakespeare does this to create particular meaning and effect for Elizabethan audience.

QUOTATIONS TO CONSIDER:

"A pair of star cross'd lovers"

- Star crossed lovers implies that their fates have already been chosen, and that fate has a tragic ending.

"I fear too early, for my mind misgives / Some consequences yet hanging in the stars"

- Romeo is thinking of attending the Capulet's party. Stars are referenced to symbolise Romeo's destiny. He knows that attending the Capulet's party could have major consequences.

"O, swear not by the moon, th' inconstant moon"

- Juliet uses celestial imagery to tell Romeo that he needs to be sure that his love for her is true. His love cannot be changing like the phases on a moon.

Question 10

- Shakespeare deals with the concept of love throughout the play. The meaning, causes and impact surrounding love are all explored in *Romeo and Juliet*, and Shakespeare does this successfully through his use of language, style and imagery.

- The developing relationship between Romeo and Juliet is seen right from the offset, and the audience see how their relationship impacts on all the other characters in the play.

- The best way to get a good idea about the concept of love and how, where and why it appears in the play is through examples.

- Explore the different types of love such as love at first sight, young love, true love, courtly love, sexual love, traditional love etc.

QUOTATIONS TO CONSIDER:

"For I ne'er saw true beauty until tonight"

- It's powerful, exciting and demonstrates the idea of young love.

"She's way to young to be a bride"

- Juliet is represented as headstrong and passionate.

"Thus with a kiss I die"

- This reinforces the strength in Romeo's love for Juliet. The fact that both characters are willing to die in order to be together shows this idea of true love.

"Don't waste your love on somebody, who doesn't value it"

- This signifies that love is a meaningful and powerful feeling which should not be passed around easily. Shakespeare suggests that love needs to be treasured and handed out only to people who truly love you back.

"My only love sprung from my only hate"

- This highlights that Romeo and Juliet's relationship would be forbidden by their families. Their love for another implies further conflict as the audience are fully aware that their families are rivalries.

IMPROVE YOUR ENGLISH ABILITY!

FURTHER YOUR LEARNING!

How2Become have created these FANTASTIC guides to help you fully prepare for GCSE Maths.